Demetrius Augustine Gallitzin

A Defence of Catholic Principles in a lLtter to a Protestant Clergyman

Fourth Edition

Demetrius Augustine Gallitzin

A Defence of Catholic Principles in a ILtter to a Protestant Clergyman
Fourth Edition

ISBN/EAN: 9783744687423

Printed in Europe, USA, Canada, Australia, Japan

Cover: Foto ©Lupo / pixelio.de

More available books at **www.hansebooks.com**

A DEFENCE

OF

CATHOLIC PRINCIPLES,

IN A

LETTER TO A PROTESTANT CLERGYMAN.

TO WHICH IS ADDED,

AN APPEAL TO THE PROTESTANT PUBLIC

BY THE REV. DEMETRIUS A. GALLITZIN.

FOURTH EDITION.
Corrected and Enlarged with the permission of the Author.

NEW YORK:
THE CATHOLIC PUBLICATION SOCIETY.
1880

ENTERED according to the Act of Congress, in the year 1837, by F. LUCAS, JR. in the Clerk's Office of the District Court of Maryland.

CONTENTS.

Preface, ... 5
A Defence, &c. 7
Article I.—A Summary of the Catholic Doctrine, 13
Art. II.—Confession, . 46
Art. III.—The Eucharist or Lord's Supper, 56
Art. IV.—The Sacrifice of the Mass, 84
Art. V —Communion under one Kind or Form, 92
Art. VI.—Purgatory and Prayers for the Dead, 98
Art. VII.—Honouring the Saints, and applying to
    their Intercession, . 112
Art. VIII.—Images, Pictures and Relics, 129
Art. IX.—The Pope, . . 140
Art. X.—Toleration, . . 158
Conclusion, ... 169
An Appeal to the Protestant Public, 184

PREFACE.

A SERMON preached by a Protestant minister on a day appointed by government for humiliation and prayer, in order to avert from our beloved country the calamity of war, was the occasion of the present letter.

The professed subject of this sermon on such a day, was, or should have been, to excite his hearers to humility and contrition, and to a perfect union of hearts and exertions, during the impending storm; but he, very likely alarmed at a much greater danger, of which nobody else but himself dreamed; alarmed I mean, and trembling for the ark of Israel, likely to be carried off by those Philistines, called Roman Catholics; or alarmed, perhaps, at the very probable danger of an intended invasion from the pope, who would, to be sure, avail himself of the confused state of the country, to assist his English friends in the conquest of it, that he might by that means, extend his jurisdiction; or, in fine, alarmed, perhaps, lest our treacherous Catholics would take advantage of the times, and by forming a new gunpowder plot, blow up the congress hall, state houses, and all the Protestant meeting houses of the United States; alarmed at least, by something or other, he suddenly forgets his subject, and putting on a grave countenance, enters the most solemn caveat against his popish and heathen neighbours, cautions his hearers against their superstitions, and gives them plainly enough to understand, that such popish neighbours are not to be considered their fellow-citizens.

It is no small source of astonishment to see in a country so liberal, polished, and enlightened as the United States of America, a continuation of violent attacks, unjust prejudices, and foul calumnies against the Roman Catholic Church. As attacks of this kind are so very common, and generally proceed too evidently from ignorance or impotent rancour, to merit attention, I have always treated them hitherto with silent contempt—the present one I have thought necessary to notice, both as it proceeded from a respectable quarter, and as I judged that silence, if invariably observed, would be construed by many into an admission of the charges alleged against us. I expected, at first, that a few respectful lines, which I published in a gazette, would have been sufficient to draw from the gentleman an apology for his uncharitable expressions. I found myself deceived in my expectation. After having waited in vain from September, until some time in the winter, I made up my mind to send the gentleman the following Defence of Catholic principles.

A DEFENCE, &c.

Dear Sir,

AFTER your unprovoked attack upon the whole body of Roman Catholics, it was expected that an apology for the same would have been considered by you as due to them. To exhibit above one hundred and fifty millions of Catholics,*

* The number of one hundred and fifty millions will not appear exaggerated to any one who considers, that Italy contains nearly twenty millions of Catholics; France, upwards of thirty millions; that Spain, Portugal, Austria, Bohemia, Hungary, Belgium, Ireland, Poland, South America, and some parts of North America, viz: Cuba, Mexico, Lower Canada, &c. are inhabited almost exclusively by Catholics; that they are numerous in the United States, and still more so in the Protestant kingdoms of Europe, for instance, five millions in the dominions of the king of Prussia; that there are flourishing churches and missions in Turkey, throughout the vast continents of Asia and Africa, in the islands of the Pacific and the Southern Ocean; that the Phillippine Islands contain two millions, and the diocess of Goa alone, nearly half a million of Catholics. From these and other facts, we are inclined to believe that the total number above mentioned, instead of being overrated, might, on the contrary, be raised to one hundred and seventy, or perhaps, one hundred and eighty millions.

NOTE.—This was written nearly fifty years ago.

who undoubtedly constitute the most numerous and imposing christian society in existence, as standing upon a level with heathens, to represent the whole of them as a superstitious set, wandering in the paths of darkness, and finally, to exclude the Catholics of the United States from their rank of citizens, cannot be considered by you as a trifling insult. Now, sir, as a gentleman, you cannot be ignorant of the common principles of civility. As a christian, and especially as a teacher of the christian religion, you cannot be ignorant of that great precept of christian charity, which our blessed Saviour declares to be the very soul of religion, on which depend the whole law and the prophets, Matt. xxii. 40. Wishing to act under the influence of those principles, I shall, according to the direction of our common Saviour, (Matt. v. 44,) return you good for evil, and pray God to bless you, whilst you are persecuting and calumniating us. And, though your alleged charges, it is true, destroy themselves, and their falsehood must be evident to any one who is even slightly acquainted with Catholic doctrines; nay, every reflecting mind should thence infer the weakness of that cause which stands in need of such aid for its support;*

---

* 'It is an observation,' says Count de Maistre, 'which I recommend to the attention of all those who think and reason: truth, when it combats error, is never angry. Amidst the immense number of our controversial works, it requires

yet, as you refuse us (what we think we are justly entitled to) an apology, and as such charges continue to be repeated, I have deemed it expedient to give you and the public an explanation of our tenets, in order to convince every candid mind, that we are not guilty of superstition.

With respect to the personal insult reflected on us from the odious colours in which we and our doctrines are exhibited, it excites in us rather compassion than anger. Our only wish is that our separated brethren may be enabled by the light of God to know the truth, and having known it, by his special assistance to embrace and follow it.

If, instead of accusing us in a general manner, you had been pleased to state distinctly in what

a microscopic eye to discover one single effusion of anger, which might escape from human weakness. Such men as Bellarmine, Bossuet, Borgier, &c. were able to dispute all their life, without suffering themselves to use, I do not say the slightest insult, but even the slightest personality. This character the Protestant writers possess in common with the Catholic, whenever they combat incredulity. The reason of it is, because, in this case, it is the Christian that is combatting the Deist, the Materialist, and the Atheist; and therefore, it is still truth refuting error. But, now, let these men only turn their arms against the church of Rome, behold, every thing at once is altered; they insult her with the grossest violence. And why? Because error is never calm, when it combats against truth. This two-fold characteristic is visible every where, as also it is every where decisive. There are few demonstrations which conscience sees more clearly.'

particular points we are guilty of superstition, a great deal of time would have been saved, as my defence would be confined to those particular points of attack; but now, not knowing those against which the attack is intended, I must be ready at all points.

In order to ascertain whether we are or not guilty of superstition, it will be necessary, in the first place, to give a distinct definition of the word superstition. Many disputes originate altogether in the misunderstanding of words, and might be entirely avoided, by first agreeing about the meaning of those words.

Such as have treated of superstition, give the following definition of it, which every one will readily grant to be correct: Superstition is an inordinate worship of the true or of a false divinity

To accuse us of superstition, then, is to say, that we either worship the true God in an ordinate manner, or that we worship false gods, or that we are guilty of both.

To which of the tenets of the Catholic Church does any of these three modes of superstition apply.

I reply boldly, to none; and in order to convince you and your hearers that I am justified in saying so, I shall give you a short sketch of our Catholic principles; but do not expect to find, maintained by them, those pretended Catholic principles which ignorance, prejudice, and I am apprehensive, sometimes malice and ill-will, falsely attribute to Catholics. Thus I shall say nothing of the pope's power to grant licenses to commit sin, or dispensations from the oath of allegiance, about the worship of saints, and many other articles falsely attributed to Roman Catholics, and which (I have too much reason to believe) are industriously propagated to answer certain selfish and iniquitous purposes.

May the great God give me grace to display before your eyes and those of the public, the beauties and perfections of the Catholic church, that in her you may behold the true and immaculate spouse of Jesus Christ, Ephes. v. 31, 32; ever subject and ever faithful to him, 24; ever loved and cherished by him, 25; that in her you may behold the kingdom of which Jesus Christ is the king, Luke i. 32; the sheepfold of which Jesus Christ is the shepherd, John x. 16; the house of the living God, 1 Tim. iii. 15; the pillar and ground of the truth, ibid; always one, John x. 16, Ephes. iv. 4, 5; always visible, Matt. v. 14; unconquerable by the united efforts of hell and earth, Matt. xvi. 18; that none may fall under the sentence pronounced by St. Peter II. ii. 12, 'these men, blaspheming what they know not, shall perish;' and by St. Jude 10, 'these men blaspheme what they krow not.' Woe to them, &c. On the contrary, that all may feel themselves compelled to exclaim with Balaam, 'How beautiful are thy tabernacles, O Jacob; and thy tents, O Israel,' Num xxiv. 5.

ARTICLE I.

A SUMMARY OF THE CATHOLIC DOCTRINE.

We believe, dear sir, that Almighty God is perfect in himself, and perfect in all his works. After creating the world and all that it contains, God saw all the things that he had made, and they were very good, Gen. i. 31. By the help of natural philosophy, anatomy, astronomy and other sciences, many of the beauties and perfections of nature, have been discovered, which give us the most exalted idea of the power and wisdom of their Creator; many more, however, are, and will remain wrapt up in mystery, and are thereby the better calculated to give us some, though faint idea, of the immensity of God. From the discoveries which have been made, we are struck with astonishment at the wonderful harmony displayed in the whole system of nature, and in every part of it. The progressive development of our faculties, the gradual, though slow advancement of knowledge, have enabled us to penetrate into a few of the secrets of nature. Every discovery has paved the way to new ones, and were the world to last millions of years, we should still discover more, and yet be obliged to own that we have scarcely obtained one drop out of an ocean. This world, sir, which we so much admire, will pass away, notwithstanding all its beauties and perfections. It was created, we believe, for the use of man during his mortal life, to afford him a comfortable and happy existence. But, sir, man is not created for this visible world alone; his body was formed of clay, and his soul, his immortal soul, is the image of God, the breath of the most high: 'And the Lord God breathed into his face the breath of life, and man became a living soul,' Gen. ii. 7. We believe that the soul of man was created for everlasting happiness, and that created to the image of God, we are to rest for ever in the bosom of God. With St. Augustine we exclaim. 'Thou hast made us for thyself, O Lord, and our hearts are restless until they repose in thee.'

We believe that, although created to the image of God, we may defile in ourselves that image, and thus remove ourselves from our original destination. We believe we shall attain the objects of our destination, only if we try to preserve in ourselves that image undefiled—or in other words if we try to be and to become more and more similar to our Creator; 'be perfect (says our Saviour) as also your heavenly Father is perfect,'

Matt v. 48. We believe then, that in order to become ripe for heaven, we must try to keep ourselves pure and undefiled, shew the most perfect obedience to our Creator, the most perfect submission of our hearts and understandings, practice humility, chastity, justice, and above all, the most perfect charity; that is, we must love God above all things, and our neighbour as ourselves. The will of God must *always* be the only rule of our conduct, we must love what he loves, hate what he hates, and with due proportion, do as he does; consequently, we must consider sin as the greatest of all evils, and be willing to sacrifice even life itself, rather than offend our Creator, by a wilful transgression of his commandments. As Almighty God is infinitely just, infinitely good to all men, even to the worst of men, so must we be strictly just and charitable to all men, even to our enemies, without distinction of believer or unbeliever, Christian or Jew, or Mahometan, or Heathen, &c. In short, sir, we believe that, in order to become saints in heaven, we must lead a holy life upon earth, and that all the external acts of religion which we practice, can never afford a substitute for a holy and virtuous life. We hear taught from all the Catholic pulpits in the world, and believe, that confidence in external acts of religion, unsupported and unaccompanied by the practice of virtue, is a most abominable presumption and real superstition.

To convince you, sir, that such is the real belief of Catholics, I refer you to all Catholic catechisms, prayer-books, meditations, sermons, in short, to all the spiritual books of any kind that ever were published in any part of the Catholic world. Being provided with books of that kind from almost every Catholic country in Europe, I readily offer them to the inspection of any person curious to ascertain the doctrine of Catholics on so important a subject, on which misrepresentation has created so many prejudices. What is more common, indeed, than to hear it said that a Catholic, or if you choose, a Papist, puts so much confidence in his priest, that it matters little to him whether he commits sin or not; for after having broken all the commandments of God, he thinks he has nothing to do but to confess his sins to the priest, and behold, from the gulf of perdition, he leaps at once into paradise!

Catholics, then, among whom there are thousands and thousands of men eminent for their genius and learning, men of the most transcendant talents, celebrated in all the different branches of literature, and what is much better, famed for the most genuine, the most heroic virtue; Catholics then, I say, are believed, or at least represented, to be most brutally stupid! But let us proceed.

We believe that man, originally created to the image of God, has in a great measure defiled that sacred image, by tasting the forbidden fruit. We believe that, in consequence of that sin which we call original sin, man fell under the curse of God, was not only driven out of the earthly paradise. but what is infinitely worse, forfeited his right and title to the happiness of heaven; and we believe that it was not in the power of man, to offer to the irritated justice of God, a satisfaction adequate to the offence. As the malice and iniquity of an offence must in a great measure be determined by the degree of dignity and elevation of the being to whom the offence is given, God being infinite in power, dignity, and perfection, the offence must be in some measure, infinite in its malice. Man, on the other hand, being limited, can have nothing to offer by way of reparation or satisfaction, but what is limited in its value, and of course, not adequate as a satisfaction. The wrath and the justice of God demanded a victim; all mankind must be sacrificed, must suffer, and their sufferings must be infinite, which they cannot be, unless they last forever, or a being equal to the offended Creator, must step forward and pay the ransom. As every act of an Infinite Being, is of infinite value, one word, one sigh, from such a Being, would be an adequate satisfaction. Here then, is the pivot upon which turns the whole christian religion, with all its profound mysteries. Mankind being doomed to eternal torments, and not being able to satisfy

God's infinite justice, within any limited period, Jesus Christ, the Son of God, equal to his Father, burning with zeal for his glory, and with love for man, offers himself as the victim of God's infinite justice. The ransom is accepted, and a new chance of heaven is offered to man.

The main point to be explained now, is, in what manner we believe that Jesus Christ has accomplished the redemption of man. This will, of course, exhibit all that Catholics believe of the church of Christ, of the christian religion, and of all its mysteries.

We believe that Jesus Christ, in order to become a victim of propitiation for our sins, assumed human nature, which being united to his Divine nature, formed one person. As God he could not suffer; but by becoming a real man, assuming a real human soul, and a real human body, he made himself liable to sufferings, and by being God, his sufferings became of infinite value, and of course, adequate as a satisfaction.

We believe that Jesus Christ was conceived in the womb of the spotless virgin Mary, by the power and operation of the Holy Ghost, Luc. i. 35.

We believe that Jesus Christ, immolating himself for our sins, acted in the capacity of a priest, a priest being the minister of a sacrifice; we believe that he is both high priest and victim, Heb v. 7, 8, 9, 10.

Mankind having fallen by original sin, into a wonderful state of depravity, the light of their reason, being almost extinguished, their understanding perverted, (witness the many ridiculous and abominable systems taught by their wise men and philosophers,) their hearts corrupted and given up a prey to all the passions, Jesus Christ came not only to satisfy for our sins, and by that means to open for us the gates of heaven, but he also came to shew both by word and example, what means we must take in order to obtain heaven.

We believe that in Jesus Christ we have a perfect example and pattern of a holy life, and an infallible teacher of salvation.

We believe that in the gospels is recorded a part, though a very small part, of what Christ did and preached during his visible existence on earth, John xxi. 25.

We believe the authors of these gospels to have been inspired by the Holy Ghost, and therefore, we believe every word contained in them, as proceeding from the fountain of truth.

As we believe the gospel of Christ to be a divine book, so we believe that none but a divine authority can expound it. We shudder at the idea of bringing that divine book before the tribunal of limited and corrupted reason, and we candidly confess that although we were provided with a greater share of wisdom and knowledge than Solo mon possessed, we should still be unequal of ourselves to the task of understanding and explaining the gospel, or other parts of Holy Writ. In this we are confirmed by St. Peter, who says that 'no prophecy of the Scripture is made by private interpretation,' 2 Peter, i. 20.

As we believe that Holy Scripture is the word of God, so we believe that Holy Scripture misinterpreted, is not the word of God, but the word of corrupted man; and that Scripture is often misinterpreted, we are obliged to believe from the assertion of St. Peter, who tells us that the unlearned and unstable wrest the Scriptures to their own perdition, 2 Peter, iii. 16; and likewise from our own observations: for as common sense tells us that the Holy Ghost cannot be the author of contradictory doctrines, so it tells us of course, that numbers of doctrines preached pretendedly from Scripture, must be false, as they stand in contradiction to other doctrines drawn from the same Scripture.

We believe that true faith is indispensably necessary to salvation.

'He that believeth not, shall be condemned.' Mark xvi. 16; and, 'without faith, it is impossible to please God,' Heb. xi. 6.

We believe that Jesus Christ, requiring faith as necessary to salvation, must have provided us with adequate means to obtain faith, that is, to believe without doubting all those things, which he has taught and instituted as necessary for salvation. If Jesus Christ has not provided us with such means, he must be a tyrant indeed; as he would require of us what we could not otherwise possibly perform.

We believe that Jesus Christ has established the holy Catholic Church for the above purpose, namely, as the supreme tribunal to regulate our faith, or in other words, to keep the precious deposite of revelation unaltered, to explain to us (without any possibility of error) the meaning of every part of Holy Writ necessary to salvation and likewise to preserve and transmit to posterity undefiled, all that part of Christ's divine doctrine, which was delivered only by word of mouth. either by Christ or by his Apostles, according to these words of St. Paul, 'therefore, brethren, stand firm, and hold the traditions which you have learned, whether by word, or by our epistle,' 2 Thess. ii. 14. We believe that the unwritten Word of God, transmitted to us by tradition, is entitled to the very same respect as the written word

We think it absurd to assert, that Jesus Christ has taught or preached nothing essential, but what is written in the few pages of the gospel. We do not find in the gospel, the instructions which Jesus Christ gave his Apostles, during the forty days that he appeared to them after his resurrection; and yet it is beyond all doubt, that Jesus Christ during these forty days, the last days he spent with his Apostles, instructed them particularly in the mysteries of his kingdom, or of his church, Acts i. 3.

These last instructions which Jesus Christ gave his Apostles, before parting, and when they were about entering on the arduous duties of the ministry, these last instructions I say, are not lost, although not recorded in the gospel. They form a part of that precious deposite entrusted to the church, and have, by an uninterrupted succession of pastors, been transmitted undefiled to our present days, and will be thus transmitted to the most remote generations, even to the consummation of time.

We believe, then, that the holy Catholic Church is the supreme judge, in matters of faith, both to determine the true sense of Scripture, and to settle our belief with regard to that part of Christ's doctrine, delivered by word of mouth.

Whenever the church has pronounced, the controversy is settled, doubts vanish, and we are as certain as if Jesus Christ himself had spoken.

This unerring authority of the church we discover, 1st, in the positive and most unequivocal promises of Jesus Christ.

2d. In the dictates of common sense.

1st. In the positive promises of Jesus Christ,

'Upon this rock I will build my church, and the gates of hell shall not prevail against it,' Matt. xvi. 18.

If the church could possibly teach damnable errors, then the gates of hell could prevail against her, contrary to the above promise. 'Go ye therefore, and teach all nations; baptizing them in the name of the Father, and of the Son, and of the Holy Ghost, teaching them to observe all things whatsoever I have commanded you; and behold I am with you all days, even to the consummation of the world,' Matt. xxviii. 19, 20.* Christ addressing his twelve Apostles on the present occasion, evidently speaks to all his ministers, successors of the Apostles, to the end of time, which, I think, needs no proof. Now, sir, upon that subject, I form the following argument, which sound

---

* The passage taken from St. Matt. ch. 28, v. 19, 20, is very forcible, and one of those which will for ever silence every artifice and subterfuge of error. In fact, those words of Almighty God, 'I am with you,' are used in a hundred places of the sacred Scriptures to designate a certain and infallible protection. See Psal. xxii. 4; Judg. vi.12; Isaiah, viii. 10. Our Lord making use of the same, wishes them to signify a similar protection with regard to his Apostles and their successors. But, how can he be said to assist the pastors of his church in so special a manner, if he permit them to deviate from the truth? How can he be said to remain with them all days to the end of the world, as he positively promises so to do, if it can ever happen to them to teach error and superstition.

logic will find correct. Christ promises that he himself will be with his Apostles, baptizing, preaching and teaching all nations, until the consummation of time: now Christ cannot tell a lie; therefore, Christ has fulfilled his promise, and consequently, during these 1815* years past, Christ has always been with his ministers, the pastors of the holy Catholic Church, and he will continue to be with them to the end of time, and will accompany and guide them, when they preach his word and administer his sacraments.

'And I will ask the Father, and he shall give you another paraclete, that he may abide with you for ever, the spirit of truth,' John xiv. 16, 17.† It appears that Christ asked his heavenly Father to

---

* Now 1580 years.

† The same observation that was applied to the above text of St. Matt. may be applied to this of St. John xiv. 16, 17. Some, perhaps, may object to it, that the prayers of our Lord have not always been efficacious, for example, that which he addressed to his heavenly Father in the garden of Olives, Matt. xxvi. 39, my Father, if it be possible, let this chalice pass from me. But, that this was a prayer merely conditional, it is easy to discover from the words which immediately follow: 'Nevertheless, not as I will, but as thou wilt.' On the contrary, that the success of his prayers made without restriction and condition, as the one referred to, John xiv. 16, 17, is infallible, he himself assures us in St. John xi. 41, 42, Father, I give thee thanks because thou hast heard me; and I know thou hearest me always.

bless his ministers, the pastors of his church, with the spirit of truth for ever; pray, sir, did Christ offer up any prayer in vain? And if his prayer was heard, how could the pastors of the church ever preach false doctrine?

'But when he, the spirit of truth, shall come, he will teach you all truth,' John xvi. 13. 'The church of the living God, the pillar and ground of the truth,' 1 Tim. iii. 15. If the church itself, as it comes out of the hands of God, is the very ground and pillar of truth, it will never want the reforming hand of corrupted man to put it right; it will always teach the truth, the whole truth, and nothing but the truth: and instead of attempting to reform this most perfect of all the works and institutions of God, you and I must be reformed by it. To quote all the texts, that prove the holy church of Jesus Christ to be infallible, or invested by Christ with a supreme and unerring authority in matters of faith, would be endless. I said that we discover this unerring authority even in the dictates of common sense. Yes, sir, common sense tells us, that the works of God are perfect in their kind. Now the church being most emphatically the work of God, it most assuredly must be perfect; the church, however, must be very imperfect indeed, if it wants the main perfection, which is our guide and director to heaven, it therefore must have that of always teaching truth, that of always supplying the wants of our limited and corrupted reason, that of always carrying before our eyes the bright and divine light of revelation.

Shew us a church which is not infallible, which owns itself fallible, wanting of course the main perfection which the church of Christ must have, and you shew us a church of corrupted man, not the church of Christ. Common sense tells us that, without an infallible tribunal, unanimity in faith is a thing impossible. Without a centre of unity, a fixed standard, an absolute and infallible tribunal, a living oracle to determine the mind, it is absolutely impossible, that men, framed as they are, should ever come to one and the same way of thinking. Whoever renounces this infallible authority of the church, has no longer any sure means to secure him against uncertainties, and to settle his doubts; he is in a sad and perplexed situation, tossed to and fro by every wind of doctrine.

We are confirmed in the above suggestions of common sense, by our observations. Unity in faith, we find no where but in the Catholic Church; above a hundred and fifty millions of Catholics, scattered over the face of the earth, are perfectly one in matters of faith. We meet from the distant parts of the globe, ignorant of one another's language, manners, customs, &c. yet our thoughts and principles about religion and its mysteries are exactly alike. Pray, sir, is that unity to be found among those, who have shaken off the authority of the church?* Since they have presumed to reform (as they call it) the Catholic Church, what do we see but one reformation upon another, hundreds and hundreds of different churches, one rising on the ruins of another, all widely different from one another, each styling herself the church of Christ, each appealing to the gospel for the orthodoxy of her doctrine, each calling her ministers, ministers of Christ, each calling the sermons of her ministers, the word of God, &c. &c.†

* 'Our articles and liturgy,' says Dr. Tomline, bishop of Lincoln, in his charge to his clergy, 1803, 'do not correspond with the sentiments of any of the reformers upon the continent, or with the creeds of any of the Protestant churches which are there established. Our church is not Lutheran—it is not Calvanistic—it is not Arminian—it is Scriptural.' Query, which did his Lordship believe the others to be, scriptural or unscriptural?

† Very striking is the conduct of Protestants with respect to the necessity of the authority of the church to settle disputes concerning faith. They have been compelled, through want of other efficacious means, to establish among themselves that authority, or rather its shadow This was particularly the case at the famous Synod of Dort. There indeed, the greater number of Calvin's followers, viz: the Gomarists, strove to crush their opponents, the Arminians, by the weight of Synodal, and even civil au

Common sense tells us, that the gospel, the written word, could not have been intended as the supreme judge, to fix our belief in matters of faith.

1st. Because it may be misunderstood.

The many contradictory doctrines, drawn from Scripture, prove that it is often misunderstood, and

thority: thus arrogating to themselves a power which they refused to acknowledge in the church, notwithstanding her incontestable claims; admitting in practice, what they denied in theory; and contradicting their principles in the face of the whole world. See Bossuet's Exposition and History of Variations, book xiv.

Nor is this, however, peculiar to the Synod of Dort. The same has taken place in the reformed churches of France, in the established church of England, and, generally, in all Protestant societies. All of them, after reviling the exercise of authority in matters of faith, as an act of tyranny, have nevertheless been reduced to resort to it themselves. In all of them, the leaders exercise over their flocks the most arbitrary despotism, and arrogate to themselves the privileges of infallibility, by requiring implicit submission of their deluded followers. A gross inconsistency, it is true; a full contradiction to the principles of Protestantism; but which shows, after all, how necessary is a living authority to settle all differences concerning matters of faith. Now, which of the two is to be preferred: the authority of a few men, who have received from God no mission whatever, and do not so much as agree amongst themselves; or the authority of the Catholic Church, who derives, through a regular succession, her claims from the Apostles, and has no other origin than that of christianity itself. See Bossuet's Exposition, and Fletcher's Controversial Sermons—note K to sermon ii even in matters which Christ declares it indispensably necessary for salvation. Witness the following:

'Except a man be born again, of water and the Holy Ghost, he cannot enter into the kingdom of God,' Joan. iii. 5.

'Unless you eat the flesh of the Son of man, and drink his blood, you shall not have life in you,' Joan vi. 54.

'Without faith it is impossible to please God,' Heb. xi. 6.

You will readily acknowledge that these several texts, although directing us to do certain things as indispensably necessary for salvation, are interpreted in contradictory ways, and of course misunderstood.

Some find in the gospel the necessity of baptism for salvation; others find in it, salvation without baptism.

Some find in it the necessity of receiving the flesh and blood of Christ; others find, that Christ gave us nothing but bread and wine, as memorials of his death.

Some find in the gospel that faith alone will save; others find in the gospel, the insufficiency of faith alone.

Some find in the gospel absolute and unconditional predestination; others reject it as impious and blasphemous.

Now, sir, are all these right? Or, will it be said, that it is immaterial which of these contradictory opinions we embrace? No, sir, common sense tells us that Holy Writ was not given us to be misunderstood, that when misunderstood, it leads us astray, whereas it was intended to guard us against the misfortune of being led astray. Common sense tells us then, that Scripture being a dead letter, a dumb book, which cannot explain itself, Christ must have provided some visible and living authority, some supreme and unerring tribunal, to explain Scripture, and that this is and can be no other than the church.

Otherwise, Jesus Christ, the uncreated wisdom, would have acted less wisely than human legislators, who indeed do not establish laws, without establishing tribunals to explain them. So much the less wisely, as the Holy Scriptures are in several parts full of obscurity: witness St. Peter, who says of the epistles of St. Paul: 'in which are some things hard to be understood, which the unlearned and unstable wrest, as also the other Scriptures to their own destruction,' 2 Pet. iii. 16. Witness also the difference, and even contrariety of expositions, given by Protestants themselves, on points of the greatest importance.

A second reason, why Scripture cannot be our supreme judge in matters of faith, is, because there are many that cannot read.

A third reason is: the gospels and epistles were not written for many years after the church of Christ was established and spread among many nations. For many hundred years after that, the art of printing not having been discovered, the Holy Scripture could not have been in the hands of many persons; and yet during that time the precious deposite of faith was as well kept as it has been since Holy Writ is in the hands of every body. Yes, sir, and better; every body cannot read, but every body, learned or unlearned, can submit to the church, transmitting to both, by the assistance of the Holy Ghost, the doctrine of Christ uncorrupted and in its primitive purity. Here, sir, is a mode of instruction adapted to every body's capacity.

A fourth reason: if I must take up my creed by reading Scripture, I must be convinced that the book which is put into my hands, and called the Holy Scripture, is really the genuine Scripture, as written by the Apostles; I, a poor illiterate man, not having enjoyed the benefit of a liberal education, hardly acquainted with my own language, how shall I know whether the English Bible which you put into my hands is a faithful translation of the original Hebrew and Greek or not. I shall have to take your word for it! If I do, my faith then is pinned to your sleeve. But no, sir, I cannot submit to do so, because I find material differences in different translations of the Scriptures; of course, I am kept in suspense, if I know of none but a barely human authority in support of each of the different translations.

A fifth reason is: that the Bible alone affords no security as to faith. For, it is not only concerning the fidelity of the translations, and the true sense of the Scriptures, that Protestants should entertain the most perplexing doubts; but, they should do the same concerning the very authenticity and inspiration of that sacred volume—Catholics, indeed, have not yet received a satisfactory answer, nor will such an answer, consistently with the principles of Protestantism, ever be given to the following questions: how do you know that the different books of the Bible are authentic; how do you know that all of them, and no other books, are to be received as sacred; why do you admit neither more nor less than four gospels? &c. &c.

Here Protestants cannot appeal to the Scriptures themselves, because this would be to beg the question, and, moreover, the Scriptures are silent on these points.

Neither can they appeal to the testimony of past ages; because they reject the authority of tradition with that of the church, and, in their opinion, the testimony of any body of men is fallible.

Nor to the contents of the sacred books, viz:

prophecies and divine revelations; because most of these books are merely historical or moral. Moreover, this would suppose as proved, the very fact which is to be proved, viz: the authenticity of the Scriptures.

Nor to the holy doctrine which they contain, nor to the wonderful effects produced by them; for, the Spiritual Combat, the Following of Christ, the Sinner's Guide, &c. contain a most pious doctrine, and have produced most happy effects in innumerable souls; nevertheless, they are, by no means, considered as divine and sacred.

Nor, in fine, to a certain interior light, or illustration of the Holy Ghost. The obscurity or simplicity of several books of the Old and New Testament, the difference of opinions among Protestants on the canonicity of some others; in a word, both good sense and experience show that this last reason is to be rejected as quite unfounded, as a mere illusion.

Thus it is that Protestants who cease not to appeal to the Bible, cannot according to their principles, be confident of its divinity, and find themselves stopped at the very outset. Still they admit the Bible: but why, and on what grounds? Is it sufficient of itself without the four great characteristics of the church, viz: Unity, Holiness, Catholicity, and Apostolicity; and is it conformable to the great maxim of Protestantism. according to which every body of men is liable to err or?

A sixth reason is: that on examining the conduct of Protestants, I find it quite at variance with their principles. A Protestant, to be consistent, must neither believe nor disbelieve any thing which he has not previously discussed. Hence, I would reasonably suppose, that he has compared his religion with all others that differ from it, and consequently, is convinced that his own religion is divine, and all others merely human institutions. But on the contrary, I find that with very few exceptions, the Protestant believes as he does, because accident has placed him in the society of Protestants. For after having rejected the tradition of the universal church, he, with strange inconsistency, implicitly submits to the yoke of the particular tradition of the society to which he happens to belong. This, properly speaking, is the only guide of all or nearly all* of the reformed

---

* As for those amongst the Protestants, who, like the Methodists, Quakers, &c. have adopted for their rule of faith immediate and private inspiration, they do nothing but wander still farther from the right path. For, is it not evident, that such a system is mere fanaticism; quite contrary to every idea which we ought to entertain of the wisdom of God, and of his providence with respect to his church; capable of producing as many sects as it has professors, and of leading men into every error and superstition? The experience of all ages, from the time of Montanists down to our own days, evidently confirms what we here assert.

sects, with regard to every part of their doctrine. In fact, before reading the Holy Scriptures, in order to form his faith, a Protestant, whether he be a Calvinist, an Episcopalian, or a Lutheran, has his belief already formed by the catechism which he learned from his childhood, as well as by the discourses with which his ears have constantly been greeted at home, at school, and in church. When he opens the sacred volume for the first time, he cannot fail to find in every text, the sense commonly affixed to it in his society. The opinions which he has already imbibed, are for him the dictates of the Holy Ghost. If he chanced to understand the Scriptures in any other sense, and dared maintain his private interpretation, he would be excommunicated, proscribed, and treated as a heretic.

Such has ever been the conduct of heretics since the first ages. 'Those who advise us to examine,' says Tertullian, 'wish to draw us after them. As soon as we have become their followers, they establish as dogmas, and prescribe with haughtiness, what they had before feigned to submit to our examination,' de Praescript, cap. 8. Would not one imagine that Tertullian intended to portray the Reformers thirteen hundred years before their birth?

Another proof that the belief of Protestants is founded upon their particular tradition, is that they repeat, even in our days, the arguments, the impostures, and the calumnies of the first pretended Reformers, although a thousand times refuted, and they believe them as the word of God himself.

These are sufficient reasons to induce us to believe that Holy Writ (although certainly God's word) was not intended to be our supreme judge in matters of faith ; and to convince us that Christ has provided us with a living, visible and supreme authority, to settle all our doubts with regard to the true translation of the Scripture, the true sense of it, and likewise with regard to many other essential matters not to be found in Holy Writ, but delivered by tradition. We believe then, that the Catholic Church is this living, visible and supreme authority; and if we are asked where we believe this authority resides ; we answer, in the body of Christ's ministers, the pastors of the Catholic Church, united with their head, the Roman Pontiff, and the lawful successors of those pastors, whom Jesus Christ appointed, and invested with full authority to discharge the functions of his ministry. To that body of pastors we look for heavenly instructions, in them we see the legates of Jesus Christ, invested by him with the same authority that he himself had received from his heavenly Father, 'As the Father hath sent me, I also send you,' John xx. 21.

In them we behold the organs of the Holy Ghost, 'he that heareth you, heareth me,' Luc. x. 16. 'And I will ask the Father, and he shall give you another paraclete, that he may abide with you *forever*, the spirit of truth,' John xiv. 16, 17. 'But when he, the spirit of truth, shall come, he will teach you all truth,' John xvi. 13.

Dear sir, are we then guilty of superstition in putting full confidence in these assertions and promises of Christ, and in thus believing that the spirit of truth never has departed, and never will depart from the pastors of Christ's church? In our pastors we behold men invested with the keys of the kingdom of heaven; that is, with the power of administering absolution or the forgiveness of our sins, Matt. xvi. 19, xviii. 18, and John xx. 23 To them we apply, and from their hands we receive our heavenly and spiritual food, the sacred flesh and blood of Jesus Christ, which he enjoins us to receive, John vi. 48, 59; and which he empowers his ministers to procure for us, Luke xxii. 19.

Can it be superstition, dear sir, to believe that our pastors are really in possession of the power, which Christ himself asserts he gave them, and which he promises shall remain with them forever? Since Jesus Christ has pledged his sacred veracity for the existence of those several powers in the pastors of his church, and since he has likewise promised, that the very fountain of truth, the Holy Ghost, shall be, and shall remain with those pastors for ever; we should think ourselves guilty of a great sin, if we refused the submission of either our understanding or will, to their decisions and their precepts, and of a most daring presumption, and diabolical pride, if we would, even for one moment, permit our limited reason to sit in judgment over the decisions and precepts of those, whom Jesus Christ thus declares to oe guided by the Holy Ghost for ever.

Seeing then that the pastors of the church of Christ, have always been secured by the infinite power of God, against the danger of being themselves led astray, and of leading those under their care astray into false and erroneous doctrines, we rest secure under their guidance, and knowing that the understanding of the most transcending genius can never penetrate into the mysteries of the Most High, we, both learned and unlearned, take the easy and only safe way of submission, that path in which Holy Writ assures us, that the very fools cannot err, Isa. xxxv. 8.

It is perhaps necessary to observe, that we do not believe this unerring authority to reside in any individual pastor. No: the pope himself, the successor of St. Peter, and the supreme pastor of the Catholic Church, is not by any article of Catholic communion believed to be infallible

This unerring authority is by all Catholics believed to reside in the body of the pastors, united with their head. If it does not reside there, it resides no where on earth; and the plain promises of Christ are made void, and we left to be 'tossed to and fro by every wind of doctrine,' which Christ meant to prevent by the establishment of pastors, Ephes. iv. 11, 12, 13, 14.

If we are asked how a body of sinful and fallible men, can give infallible decisions? We answer, by the power of God.

How can there be life in a lump of clay? We find the answer in Genesis ii. 7. 'And the Lord God breathed into his face the breath of life, and man became a living soul.'

How can there be infallibility in the decisions of a body of fallible men? We find the answer in John xx. 22. 'He (Jesus Christ) breathed on them, and he said to them, receive ye the Holy Ghost,' &c. &c.

'The weak things of the world hath God chosen, that he may confound the strong,' 1 Cor. i. 27.

We readily grant, that men, even the most learned, are fallible and subject to errors, whilst depending upon their reason, and their learning alone; and for this reason we believe, that not even the most extraordinary talents, improved by the most liberal education that can be obtained upon earth, will ever alone qualify a man for a minister of Christ, a pastor of souls, a spiritual guide to heaven; to pilot us surely and securely through the raging billows of a tempestuous sea, into the harbour of eternal peace. No, dear sir, this would be for the blind to lead the blind: for, if after nearly six thousand years of unrelenting exertions, human wisdom and philosophy have not been able to penetrate into one of the millions of secrets of this material world, which in a short time will be destroyed by fire: how much less can the limited understandings of even the most elevated geniuses penetrate into the dark recesses of God's sanctuary, where all is mystery? How much less, I say, can they comprehend and explain the profound mysteries of this spiritual world, the church, created for the soul of man, which is to last for ever and ever, so long as God shall be God.

Here, then, God in his mercy interposes his infinite power. Wishing to give us sure guides to lead us safely into the harbour of eternal life, Jesus Christ, God-man, by infusing his Holy Spirit of truth into those fallible men, whom he appoints his successors in the ministry, and promising never to take that spirit from them again, supplies at once the want of that knowledge which no genius, no talents, no education, ever will be able to give.

The body of pastors then, being guided by the Holy Ghost, every individual pastor draws his knowledge from that body, from the whole church. The most learned among them is willing to say with Jeremiah the prophet, 'A, a, a, Lord God, behold, I cannot speak, for I am a child,' Jer. i. 6 He is willing to acknowledge the depth of those mysterious truths of religion, in the investigation of which he must stumble at every step, unless directed by an unerring guide. Thus he applies to the decisions of the church, for the true sense of Holy Writ, for the true doctrine of Christ delivered by tradition, for the knowledge of all those tenets of religion necessary to be known for salvation. Thus, the pastor himself is led, and he is fit to be a pastor only, because he is led by an infallible guide, and instead of consulting his limited and fallible reason, in the interpretation of Scripture, instead of delivering from the pulpit his opinions of the sense of Scripture, and calling such fallible opinions the Word of God, he gives no instruction to his flock, but what he derives from the decisions of the church, guided by the Holy Spirit of truth. Thus thousands and hundreds of thousands of pastors, scattered over the whole globe, of different nations and tongues, deliver to their respective flocks one and the same doctrine, on all the different parts and mysteries of religion, and this doctrine they deliver not as opinions, but as a matter of certainty; as certain as that God is God. Is it not a pity that things.

on which our salvation essentially depend, should be only matters of opinion? It is my opinion, says one, that children may be saved without baptism; it is my opinion, says another, that God is too merciful to damn souls for ever; I think, says another, that it is immaterial what a person believes, or what religious creed he adopts, so he leads a good life. It is your opinion! And you think! Pray, are you certain? And if you are not certain in matters of such weight, how can you be happy? Good God! Will you leave it to the day of judgment to disclose whether you are right or wrong? Or, will you not rather renounce that fallible guide, your limited and corrupted reason, which never can give certainty in matters of revelation, and apply for spiritual knowledge to the fountain of eternal truth, the holy Catholic Church, guided by the Holy Ghost, that you may no longer feed on opinions and uncertainties, but repose in the bosom of certainty.

The true minister of Christ, dear sir, speaking in the name of his Divine Master, must speak with authority, with certainty, without any hesitation, on all the different mysteries of religion, on which he is obliged to instruct his flock. Wo to the wretch who shall deliver his private opinions, his own uncertain notions as the Word of God; and thus often give poison for wholesome food, the productions of weak and corrupted reason for divine revelations.

The idea which we have of a minister of Christ, you will perceive is precisely the same that the first christians must have had. Surely, dear sir, the church in 1815 must be the same as it was in the beginning: the same kind of pastors, provided with the same powers, administering the same baptism, the same eucharist or Lord's supper, in short, all the same sacraments, and preaching the same doctrine. For the words of God are unchangeable, Mark xiii. 31; his promises, infallible, 2 Cor. i. 20; his gifts, without repentance, Rom. xi. 29. Jesus Christ intended not to establish different churches, but only one, which being once founded, should last with the same faith, the same prerogatives, the same government, until the end of the world.

The Apostles of Christ, scattered over the globe, preached one and the same doctrine, because Christ was with them, Matt. xxviii. 19, 20.

The ministers of Christ in 1815, scattered over the globe, preach likewise one and the same doctrine, because Christ is still with them.

'I am with you all days, even to the consummation of the world.' Matt. xxviii. 19, 20.

The Apostles of Christ received the confessions of the faithful. 'And many of those who believed, came confessing and declaring their deeds.'

Acts xix. 18. They had received from Jesus Christ the power of forgiving and retaining sins, John xx. 22, 23.

The ministers of Christ in 1815, likewise hear the confessions of the faithful, because they have no idea that Christ ever deprived them of that power.

The Apostles of Jesus Christ proposed as infallible the decisions of the whole church, because they knew the church to be guided by the Holy Ghost; witness the first council held at Jerusalem, which settled the question about circumcision; to the decisions of which all submitted.

'It has seemed good to the Holy Ghost and to us, to lay no further burthen upon you than these necessary things.' 'He (Paul) went through Syria and Cilicia, confirming the churches: commanding them to keep the precepts of the Apostles and the ancients,' Acts xv. 28, 41. And again, 'As they passed through the cities, they delivered unto them the decrees for to keep, that were decreed by the Apostles and ancients who were at Jerusalem,' Acts xvi. 4.

The ministers of Christ in 1815, likewise submit to the decisions of the general councils of the church, because they know that the Holy Ghost is as much with the church in 1815, as he was immediately after her institution. 'I will ask the Father, and he shall give you another paraclete, that he may abide with you for ever,' John xiv. 16.

In short, sir, we do not conceive why less spiritual powers should be attributed to the ministry of Christ in 1815, than in the year 100 or 300, &c. &c. for at all times, and in all ages, the ministry is, most assuredly, intended for the same functions, as is evident from Matt. xxviii. 19, 20.

A minister of Christ in 1815, is a preacher of the *truth*, as well as in the year 100, and the *truth*, in 1815, is certainly the same, as in the year 100. 'Some, indeed, he gave to be Apostles, and some Prophets, and others Evangelists, and others Pastors and Teachers, for the perfecting of the saints, for the work of the ministry, for the edifying of the body of Christ: until we all meet in the unity of faith, &c. Eph. iv. 11, 12, 13.

A minister of Christ in 1815, is a minister of reconciliation, as well as in the year 100. You will readily allow, that men in 1815, are sinners as well as in former years, and therefore stand as much in need, as in former years, of those heavenly means and remedies, which our blessed Lord sent his Apostles to administer. 'Go ye, therefore, and teach all nations, baptizing them in the name of the Father, and of the Son, and of the Holy Ghost,' Matt. xxviii. 19. 'Whose sins you shall forgive, they are forgiven them; and whose sins you shall retain, they are retained,' John xx. 23. 'Let a man look upon us as ministers of Christ, and the dispensers of the mysteries of

God,' 1 Cor. iv. 1. Thus by baptism, they, in 1815, wipe away the stain of original sin, as well as Christ's immediate successors did. Thus also, by absolution, in 1815, they wipe away the stain of actual sin, as well as the ministers first appointed by Christ. It cannot be conceived, that Jesus Christ should grant the power of forgiving sins merely in favour of a single generation, and should then (as if repenting of that grant) deprive all future generations of the same favour and benefit; neither can it be believed, as there is not a word from the mouth of Christ in favour of such a belief. We believe then (even from the written word, without reference to the decision of the church,) that all the spiritual powers, originally granted by Christ to his ministers, still continue with his ministers, and will to the consummation of time. And we believe that any one, not in possession of those spiritual powers, which Christ himself declares he gave his ministers, cannot be a minister of Christ; he may be a gentleman, he may be a man of learning, he may be what you please, but most assuredly he cannot be a minister of Christ. I shall thank you, dear sir, to point out to me, how, in thus believing, we are guilty of superstition.

Having explained to you, what we believe of the church and the ministry of Jesus Christ, I shall now, in a brief manner, lay before you some of the particular tenets of the holy Catholic Church, those I mean which distinguish that church from all others. I begin with confession.

ARTICLE II.

CONFESSION.

This I know is the great stumbling block for all those, who, within the last three hundred years, have separated from the holy Catholic Church. We believe that the ministers of Christ, those whom we call bishops and priest, have received the power of forgiving and retaining sins, which was given to the Apostles according to John xx. 22, 23.

Pray, sir, is it superstition to believe that our omnipotent and merciful God is as able and as he was willing to continue that power in 1815, as he was, to give it to his first ministers.

If we believed that man, by his own power, could forgive sin, you would be very justifiable in accusing us of superstition; for who can forgive sins but God, or he who has received that power from him.

We believe that confession is necessarily deducible from the grant of the above power. It cannot be conceived how a minister of Christ is to exercise his power of forgiving or retaining sins, unless he has an exact knowledge of the state of the sinner's conscience; this knowledge no one can give him but the sinner himself, as probably ninety-nine out of a hundred are sins concealed from the public eye, sins of thoughts, or desires, &c.

The minister of Christ forgives in the name and by the power of Christ; but, he cannot grant absolution of the sins confessed to him without a moral certainty, that such is the inward state of the sinner, such his repentance, such his purpose of amendment, such his willingness to make restitution of property, character, &c. as to entitle him to the mercy of God, and to forgiveness from above.

The objections made against confession and the power of forgiving sins, are so futile, the benefits arising from that sacred institution so manifold and so solid, that it cannot be conceived how so many thousands were and are willing to be deprived of so valuable a blessing.

These benefits are so great, that even some of the most relentless enemies of the church could not refuse their encomiums to that holy institution. 'There is not, perhaps, a 'wiser institution,' says Voltaire in his remarks on the tragedy of Olympia.'

This Voltaire, the greatest enemy that the church

ever had, who spent his life in ridiculing the holy Scriptures and all the institutions of Christ, who declared an open war against Christ; this Voltaire, at the age of eighty odd, when in his last sickness, sent for a priest to make his confession to him. 'Confession is an excellent thing,' says the Philosophical Dictionary, 'a curb to inveterate wickedness. In the remotest antiquity, confession was practiced in the celebration of all the ancient mysteries; we have imitated and sanctified this wise practice. It is excellent to induce hearts, ulcerated by hatred, to forgive, and to make thieves restore what they have unjustly taken from their neighbour.' The Lutherans of the Confession of Augsburg, have preserved that salutary institution. Luther himself would not suffer it to be abolished. 'Sooner (says he) would I submit to the Papal tyranny, than let confession be abolished.' Collection of Luther's German writings, vol. 3, p. 272.

We find the precept of confession given by Almighty God to his chosen people.

'Say to the children of Israel, when a man or woman shall have committed any of all the sins that men are wont to commit, and by negligence, shall have transgressed the commandment of the Lord, and offended, they shall confess their sin, and restore the principal itself, and the fifth part over and above,' &c. Numb. v. 6, 7.

It does not appear that the power of forgiving

sins had been granted by Almighty God to the ministers of the old law. The confession ordered to be made under the law of Moses, may then be considered as a preparation and a figure of that required under the law of grace, which we call sacramental confession, as by the power of God and the merits of Christ, it has the grace of forgiveness and reconciliation annexed to it.

We find the practice of confession in the begining of christianity. 'And many of those who believed, came confessing and declaring their deeds.' Acts xix. 18.

We cannot believe that they came to boast of their good deeds; and therefore we understand that they confessed their bad deeds, commonly called sins.

All the holy fathers of the church, from the earliest dawn of christianity, bear ample testimony to the general practice of confession. It is difficult to conceive how any man could ever have persuaded mankind to submit to a practice so repugnant to flesh and blood, so mortifying to pride, so humiliating to human nature. The universality of this practice, to which the most powerful kings and emperors, the most renowned military commanders, the most exalted geniuses in all ages, and in all parts of the world, have cheerfully submitted, establishes in our minds a conviction beyond the possibility of a doubt, that confession owes its origin to the founder of christianity.*

The objections against sacramental confession, I repeat it, are so futile, so trifling, as hardly to deserve any answer.

First objection. How can man forgive sins?

I answer, by the power of God.

---

* With respect to the belief of the early ages, concerning the divine institution of confession, it will be sufficient to quote a few authorities. Remember, says Tertullian, that Christ left the keys of heaven to St. Peter, and through him to the church, Scorpiaci, cap. 10.

God, says St. Chrysostom, has not given to angels the power which he has given to priests, who not only regenerate, but afterwards receive the power of forgiving sins, Lib. iii. de Sacerdotio. It would be needless to quote Origen in Psal. xiii; St. Cyprian, de Lapsis, cap. 12; St. Ambrose, Lib. de Poenitentia, cap. 2 and 8, and many others. I will now cite a passage from Henry viii. in his Defence of the Sacraments against Luther, not so much from any importance to be attached to his authority, as from the reasons which he adduces, being obvious to common sense. Though confession, says he, should not have been mentioned, nor even a word said about it by the holy fathers, yet, when I see so great a multitude, for so many ages, confessing their sins to priests, I cannot believe nor think otherwise than that the practice was not introduced by human contrivance, but clearly instituted by a divine precept. Confession, therefore, notwithstanding what Luther may say, appears to me, to have been established, not by any custom of the people, nor by the institution of the fathers, but by God himself

I answer again with our blessed Saviour; 'That you may know that the *Son of man* hath power on earth to forgive sins,' &c. Matt. ix. 6. He does not say, 'That you may know that the *Son of God* has power on earth to forgive sins;' to give us to understand that this power, essentially belonging to God alone, is here communicated to man, the minister of God by excellence, and exercised by him in his own person; and again exercised by him in the persons of his ministers, as he sends them, most assuredly, to do what he did, to preach as he did, to administer reconciliation as he did, &c. 'All power is given to me in heaven and in earth.' Why this preamble, if he did not mean to give them a supernatural power? 'Go ye therefore,' &c. &c. Matt. xxviii. 18, 19. 'And receive ye the Holy Ghost; whose sins you shall forgive; they are forgiven,' &c. John xx. 22, 23.

Second objection. The institution of confession is a great encouragement to sin, as Papists think they have nothing to do, in order to obtain forgiveness, but to relate their sins to a priest.

Answer. The institution of confession misrepresented, is an encouragement to sin—granted; but surely, sir, to form a sound judgment on Catholic doctrines, it is not to polluted sources you will apply. I do not know the Protestant writer who represents them fairly; yet, it is beyond all doubt, that almost all the knowledge which Protestants have of Catholic principles, is derived from Protestant books. And pray what do they all say? Beware of Catholic books, beware of popish priests, beware of priestcraft, beware of popish superstition; thus not one Protestant out of a hundred ever has an opportunity of knowing the genuine Catholic principles.—As Fletcher very justly observes; the little knowledge which the Protestant possesses of our religion is borrowed entirely from the declamations of pulpit violence, and the misrepresentations of interested prejudice. In general, Catholic principles are exhibited in all the dark colourings of malevolence, and in all the ludicrous shapes of low ribaldry. In Dryden's words:

'A hideous figure of their foes they draw,
Nor lines, nor looks, nor shades, nor colours true,
And this grotesque design expose to public view,
And yet the daubing pleases!'

To return to the second objection, I say that confession, far from being an encouragement to sin, is the greatest check, and the greatest remedy against sin.

It is in confession that the sinner discovers to the minister of Christ, the physician of his soul, all his spiritual maladies, his weaknesses, his temptations, his inclinations, his doubts, the scruples of his conscience, his apprehensions, &c and it is there he finds comfort, encouragement, advice, instructions, remedies against temptations, in short, every thing that is necessary to cause him to forsake the ways of perdition, and with the prodigal son, to return to his father; it is there, sir, he is told of his obligations—it is there he is made sensible of the impossibility of obtaining forgiveness, unless he restores what he got by stealing, cheating, usury, or by any kind of injustice, unless he is reconciled with his adversary, unless he forsakes the occasion of sin. It is there he is reminded of the vanity of earthly pleasure, of the shortness of time, of the dreadful punishments prepared for sinners by the infinite justice of God, and of the incomprehensible blessings which the mercy of God has prepared for his saints. It is there, that in the most pathetic strains, the minister of Christ exhorts the sinner to sincere repentance, and exhibits before his eyes the merits and the sacred wounds of his dying Saviour, to rouse his desponding confidence. Ah! sir, is this encouragement to sin? Is this superstition? Great God! your wrath must have been provoked to a very high degree by the abominable sins committed on this polluted earth, when you permitted so many thousands of sinners to be deprived of so valuable a blessing as that derived from sacramental confession.

Yes, sir, many thousands of sinners, and of the most abandoned sinners, have been reclaimed in the tribunal of penance, and by the pious exertions of Christ's ministers brought back to the practice of virtue. There have been instances of sinners dying in the confessional, their hearts breaking with grief at the thoughts of having had the misfortune to offend their merciful God and Saviour. Thus, according to Christ's declaration, Luc. vii. 47, in one moment they expiated, by the perfection of their love, the sins of many years.

I shall here add one remark made by the celebrated author of the Philosophical Catechism.

'A thing well worth observing (says he) and really supernatural and miraculous is the seal or secret of confession, entrusted every day to thousands of priests, some of whom, alas! ill qualified for their profession, and capable of any other prevarication, and yet so faithfully kept. Scarcely can ALL church history, during a period of more than eighteen hundred years, furnish one example of infidelity in this point, even among those who like Luther and Calvin, turned apostates to the church. If any one reflects on the inconsistency of mankind, on the curiosity of some, and the loquacity and indiscretion of others, on the nature and importance of the affairs entrusted to confessors, the revelation of which would often have astonishing effects, on the means which various interests, avarice, jealousy and other passions fail not to try in order to compass their ends, &c.;

there will remain no doubt, but that God watches over the preservation of his work,' Philos. Catechism, vol. 3, chap. vii. art. 1.

I cannot forbear recommending, for your perusal, a book not very long since published in the city of New York, entitled, The Catholic Question in America.

You will there find what respect was paid to that venerable institution (sacramental confession) by a Protestant court of justice, at which presided the honourable De Witt Clinton. The Rev. Dr. Kohlman, a Catholic priest in the city of New York, was, by that sacrament, an instrument of restoring stolen property to its owner. Certain persons had been previously arrested on suspicion, and a prosecution instituted against them; and Dr. Kohlman, after restoring the stolen property to its owner, was summoned to give in evidence, and required to disclose the person or persons from whom he had received it. He, in a most respectful manner, stated to the court that not having any knowledge of the theft by any natural or common way of information, it being solely acquired by sacramental confession, it was his duty to suffer any punishment, even death itself, rather than divulge the knowledge acquired in that way. The court unanimously decided in his favour; and there being no evidence against the defendants, they were acquitted.

In that same book you will find a complete treatise on sacramental confession, wherein by the most respectable testimonies from the holy fathers, it is clearly proved that sacramental confession owes its origin to the Divine Founder of our holy religion, and has been practised from the earliest dawn of christianity, and in all ages of the church, down to our present times.

From this short explanation which I have given of the Catholic doctrine of confession, you will candidly acknowledge, dear sir, that the practice of sacramental confession, far from being superstitious, is a very useful one. I shall now explain what the Catholic Church teaches and commands us to believe with regard to the holy eucharist.

ARTICLE III.

THE EUCHARIST OR LORD'S SUPPER.

It is sufficient to read the words of Christ in the gospel to form an accurate idea of what the Catholic Church believes on that important subject.

Jesus Christ says, 'I am the bread of life,' John vi. 35 and 48. 'I am the living bread, which came down from heaven; if any man eat of this bread, he shall live for ever; and the bread which I will give, is my flesh, for the life of the world,' John vi. 51, 52.

'Unless you eat the flesh of the Son of man, and drink his blood, you shall not have life in you. He that eateth my flesh, and drinketh my blood hath everlasting life; and I will raise him up at the last day. For my flesh is meat indeed, and my blood is drink indeed.'

'He that eateth my flesh, and drinketh my blood, abideth in me, and I in him.'

'As the living Father hath sent me, and I live by the Father; so he that eateth me, the same also shall live by me,' John vi. 54, 58.

Here you see in plain words what we believe on the subject of the eucharist.

We believe that Jesus Christ is the living bread, the food of our immortal souls, John vi. 35, 48.

We believe that we must feed on the sacred flesh and blood of Christ, in order to obtain eternal life, John vi. 54, 55.

We believe that the flesh of Christ and the blood of Christ are our spiritual food indeed, and not in figure, 56; and finally, that in the holy eucharist we receive Jesus Christ himself, the spiritual food of our souls, 58.

Divine mysteries being impervious to human reason, we do not arrogate to ourselves the right of philosophizing on the present mystery, nor do we make ourselves uneasy about the means, by which Christ is to enable us to accomplish what he here requires. We do not ask with the Jews:

How can this man give us his flesh to eat? But with Simon Peter we say, 'Lord, to whom shall we go;' thou hast the words of eternal life, John vi. 69. Surely, sir, we ought not to be blamed for believing that Christ meant what he said.

The Jew may be scandalized, the philosopher may smile in his self-sufficiency, but the Catholic, with the humility of a child, submits, not knowing what it is to reason upon impenetrable mysteries. He may stand in silent raptures of astonishment at the depth of God's unfathomable wisdom, but he does not know what it is to doubt, and he has that comfort to know, that before the tribunal of Christ he will be able to bring the very words of Christ in evidence of the orthodoxy of his belief.

Pray, sir, laying aside all prejudice, will you say that Christ, on the great day of retribution, will condemn me as guilty of superstition for believing precisely what he tells me, viz: that I must receive his living flesh and blood; that I really receive both in the blessed eucharist; that I receive Christ himself according to his own repeated declaration? You will hardly say so.

On the other hand, what excuse, what plea will any one have, who, notwithstanding Christ's positive declaration, can see nothing in the sacrament, but bread and wine?

Christ said, you must eat my flesh and drink my blood; no, no, says limited reason, for how can Christ give us his flesh to eat? Christ says, my flesh is meat indeed, and my blood is drink indeed. No, no, says corrupted reason, it cannot be so indeed, it must be meant as a figure only. Christ says: 'he that eateth me, shall live by me.' What! (says limited reason) what! eat Christ? that is absurd, that cannot be. An thus does man's corrupted reason do away and make void the sacred words of Christ, and substitute a shadow, a mere nothing, for the most precious gift which Jesus Christ ever bestowed on man.

To a superficial mind there is perhaps something specious in these dictates of limited reason. But, sir, we must remember that to understand and explain divine mysteries, is not the province of human reason. If we are justifiable in rejecting one mystery, because it is beyond the limits of reason, then we may, nay, (in order to be consistent,) we ought to reject all divine mysteries as beyond the same limits. Thus we ought to expunge from our creed the mystery of the trinity and of the incarnation, the very fundamental principles of the christian religion. Who indeed, can conceive how there are three really distinct persons in God, and every one of them God, and yet that there is but one God? Even the existence of a God invisible and immense; in every place whole and entire, and yet but one; even the existence of that God, I say, ought to be rejected, if we are justifiable in rejecting any mystery on account of its being impervious to limited reason.

Here I would beg leave to observe, that a distinction ought to be made, between a thing being against reason and being above reason. If a thing is really against sound reason, we cannot submit to believe it, neither would Almighty God require it, as in doing so, he would contradict his own work, which is impossible. If a thing is above reason, that is, beyond the limits of the human understanding: this is by no means a proof of its being false.

With regard to the present mystery, then, if it is really against sound reason, Christ cannot, and will not require a belief of it; if it is only beyond the limits of reason, it ought to be believed where the words of Christ are plain. Nay, sir, its being impervious to reason stamps on it a character of divinity, which essentially belongs to the works of God.

Revelation, similar to the pillar of fire, which guided the Israelites in the desert, has its dark side; but it has likewise its luminous side, whence emanate the purest and brightest rays of truth. In vain would human reason endeavour to penetrate into the dark recesses of the sanctuary; a veil hangs before it, and in granting us the blessing of revelation, it certainly was the will of God to supply the wants, the insufficiency of reason

It was the will of the Most High, that to him, with the most profound humility, we should make a sacrifice, not of reason itself, but of that vain and presumptuous confidence which we are too apt to have in the dictates of our limited reason. As Mr. Voltaire observes, 'reason conducts you; advance by its light, proceed a few steps more; but limit your career; on the brink of the Infinite, stop short, there an abyss begins, which you must respect.'

'The most common things (says the celebrated Locke) have their dark sides, where the most piercing eye cannot penetrate; many difficulties are found in natural religion.'

Conceive, if you can, how any thing can be created out of nothing, how God is present every where, without being confined by space; conceive what eternity is; conceive, if you can, how in a living man, soul and body are joined together. Is it a wonder then, if in revealed religion, in God's sanctuary, many mysteries are found, exceeding the reach of human comprehension, and which it would even be impious to attempt to fathom The mysteries of revelation bear no proportion to the measure of human understanding. Reason leads you to the door of the sanctuary, but there it leaves you. Reason is now silent and God speaks; man listens, and adores. He sees evidently that he should believe; he hears God distinctly dictate mysteries, which he commands him to believe and to revere; but he understands not those mysteries, which he is commanded to revere. He is even more satisfied than if he understood what forms the object of his belief: because, what man's limited understanding can comprehend, appears to be less awful, less worthy the divine greatness, than what human wisdom cannot penetrate.

To return to the mystery of the eucharist, we grant, it is, in a great measure, incomprehensible; the most learned of our divines do not pretend to comprehend it. But, sir, it is evident, that God here speaks, and that he speaks in the most unequivocal terms, that he repeatedly makes use of the very same expressions: my flesh, my blood, &c. It is evident that Christ at the last supper tells his Apostles, 'Take and eat, &c. This is my body, &c. Drink ye all of this, &c. This is my blood.' It is evident then, that we must listen and adore. A positive refusal to believe would be downright impiety. But, sir, if we permit our limited reason to sit in judgment on the mysteries of revelation, we may soon, by arbitrary interpretations, get rid of them all; and thus a belief, framed by the interpretation of limited reason, amounts to a real and positive refusal to believe. In the present instance, what could justify us in asserting, that in the eucharist nothing is given, nothing received, but bread and wine? Surely not the words of Christ, for his words and his repeated words are plainly, *my flesh, my blood;* surely not the impossibility of receiving the flesh and blood of Christ, for, it is certainly as easy for Jesus Christ to feed our immortal souls with his own flesh, as it was for him to assume that sacred flesh. It is as easy for him to conceal his sacred flesh and blood under the forms or appearances of bread and wine, as it is easy for him to conceal his glorious divinity, although every where present, from our eyes.

Surely it will not be said, that our belief is unreasonable. God is so great, so magnificent, so wonderful in his works; he has done such stupendous things for the happiness of man, that nothing how great, how mysterious, soever, proceeding from so great a God, appears to us unreasonable to believe.

Our immortal souls are the images of the eternal Father.

Our immortal souls are redeemed by the merits of the Divine Son, and washed in his sacred blood.

It is for the sake of those immortal souls, that the Divine Son assumed human flesh and blood; and during thirty-three years, was willing to lead a life of sufferings, and to subject himself to all the torments which the malice of hell and earth combined, chose to inflict upon him.

It was for the sake of our immortal souls that

the Divine Son offered his sacred flesh and blood as a victim of propitiation to be immolated on the cross.

Our immortal souls then must be truly great, truly precious, in the sight of God, when so much was done for them. Is it then unreasonable to believe, after all this, that nothing less than the flesh and blood of a God-man is found by our great and merciful God, worthy to afford spiritual food and nourishment to those immortal souls, especially as this flesh and blood by being sacrificed, became the life of those souls, which by sin were dead, to eternal life?

Will it be found unreasonable to believe, that Christ meant precisely what he said? Surely, he came to instruct and not to deceive. When he saw that the Jews were scandalized, and asked, 'how can this man give us his flesh to eat?' Was not this the opportunity to undeceive them, and to explain himself; in short, to say, 'I do not mean that you shall eat my flesh and drink my blood,' or in other words, 'I do not mean what I said.' Instead of this, we find Jesus Christ, after a double *amen*, insisting no less than six times in the most unequivocal manner upon the necessity of receiving his flesh and blood; we find Jesus Christ, at the last supper, taking bread and wine, and having blessed them, giving them to his Apostles, and saying, take ye and eat—this is my body—drink ye all of this—this is my blood, &c. We find the great St. Paul, 1 Cor. x. 16, and xi. 23, 29, making use of the very same expressions, and condemning the unworthy receiver, for not discerning the Lord's body. Surely, sir, we could not be required to discern the body of Christ, were it not in the eucharist.

We afterwards find the whole church of Christ, during eighteen centuries, that is, during almost fifteen hundred years before the pretended reformation, and three hundred after it, believing and teaching every where that the flesh and blood of Christ are received in the holy eucharist.

In the first age of the church, St. Ignatius, disciple of St. John the Evangelist, bishop of Antioch and martyr, speaks in the following manner of certain heretics of his time: 'they abstain from the holy eucharist and oblation, because they do not acknowledge the eucharist to be the flesh of our Saviour Jesus Christ, which suffered for our sins.' Epist. ad Smyrn. Therefore, it is not the mere figure of the body of Christ, as Protestants say, but his flesh itself.

In the second age, St. Justin Martyr has the following plain words. 'As Jesus Christ incarnate had flesh and blood for our salvation, so are we taught, that the eucharist is the flesh and blood of the same Jesus incarnate,' Apolog. ii. *ad Antonium.*

In the third age, St. Cyprian says, 'the bread

which our Lord gave to his disciples, being changed, not in shape, but in nature, by the omnipotence of the word, is made flesh.' *Serm. de Coena Domini.*

In the same age, the learned Origen says, 'in the old law, the manna was meat in an enigma, but now the flesh of God is meat in reality, as himself says, my flesh is meat indeed,' Hom. 1. in Levit.

In the same age again, Tertullian, the great champion and defender of the faith, says, 'the bread taken and distributed to his disciples, he made his body,' Book 4 against Marcion, ch. 40.

In the fourth age, St. Ambrose says, 'before it be consecrated, it is but bread, but when the words of consecration come, it is the body of Christ,' Book 4 of the Sacram. ch. 5.

In the same age, St. Gregory, of Nyssa, bears testimony to the same truth, 'we truly believe, even by the word of God, that the sanctified bread is changed into the body of God,' Orat. Catechist c. 37.

Also, St. Cyril of Jerusalem, in his 4th Catechetical Instruction, says, 'since Christ himself has said of the bread, this is my body, who will henceforth dispute it? And since he himself has said, this is my blood, who will dare entertain any doubt, and say, that it is not his blood? On a former occasion, he changed water into wine, at

Cana of Galilee; shall we then consider him less worthy of credit, when he changes wine into blood? Do not judge by the taste, but by faith, and be assured beyond all doubt that what appears to be bread, is not bread, but the body of Christ; and what appears to be wine, is not wine, but the blood of Christ.' Could the Doctor more clearly express the real presence, or more forcibly exclude the mere figure?

And also St. John Chrysostom, bishop of Constantinople, 'he that sits above with his Father, even in the same instant of time—gives himself to all such as are willing to receive him, &c. whereas Christ leaving his flesh to us, yet ascending to heaven, there also he hath it,' *L. de Sacerd.*

The same in his 60th homily, to the people of Antioch, has the following words:

'What pastor feeds his sheep with his own blood! but, what do I say? pastor! many mothers there are, who after having suffered the pains of labour, give their babes to strangers to nurse. This Jesus Christ would not suffer, but he feeds us himself, and that with his own blood.'

In the fifth age, St. Augustine, that great luminary of the church, and a convert from the Manichean heresy, in his sermon on the 33d Psalm, makes use of the following expressions: How David could be carried in his own hands, we find not, but in Christ we do, for he was carried in his own hands, when giving his body, he said, this is my body; for then he carried that body in his own hands,' &c.

In short, sir, it is evident, that in all ages, down to the pretended reformation, the real presence of Christ in the eucharist has been believed by all christendom. It is evident, that the same belief has continued throughout the whole Catholic world to our present days.

It is evident that such has always been, likewise, the constant belief of the eastern or Greek Church. See the testimonials of seven archbishops of the Greek Church, in a book entitled, *Perpetuite de la Foi*, vol. 3, p. 569, the testimonies of the archbishops and clergy of the Archipelago, page 572; of four patriarchs of Constantinople, of the patriarch of Alexandria, and of thirty-five metropolitans or archbishops, *anno* 1672, ch. 6, page 623; of the churches of Georgia and Mingrelia, ch. 7, page 634; of the patriarch of Jerusalem, &c. &c. Such is the faith of the Armenians, Moscorites, Surians, Cophts, Moronites, Russians, &c. &c.*

---

* These testimonies and several similar ones are to be found, not only in that learned work, La Perpetuite de la Foi, but also in the Amicable Discussion, in the letters of a Catholic doctor to a Protestant gentleman, by F. Scheffmacher, and in the Literal and Dogmatical Explanation of the Ceremonies of the Mass, by F. Le Brun. They have all the characteristics of authenticity that can be desired, being accompanied with the signatures not only of the

A DEFENCE OF CATHOLIC PRINCIPLES. 69

This truth appeared so evident to Luther himself, that he never could get over it. His words are very remarkable.

'If any man (says he) could have convinced me five years ago, that in the sacrament there is nothing but bread and wine, he had wonderfully obliged me, for with great anxiety did I examine this point, and labour with all my force to get clear of the difficulty, because by this means, I

Oriental bishops, but also of the ambassadors of different European nations.

It may be proper here to mention why and how they were obtained.

About the middle of the 17th century, the celebrated Nicolius had composed in favour of the real presence, a work, in which he adduces, among other proofs, that taken from the constant and unanimous belief of all christian churches, the reformed ones alone being excepted. As the Protestant divines continued to maintain that the eastern churches held the same belief as themselves concerning the eucharist, different ambassadors and consuls were requested to ascertain the fact. Having, agreeably to the request, made the necessary inquiries, they sent to France the professions of faith of the patriarchs, archbishops, and bishops of the different Oriental churches. All, without exception, expressed themselves in the most positive terms in favour of the real presence which they declared to be their doctrine, and complained of the calumnies heaped on them by the Calvinists who had charged them with holding the contrary; whereas, they condemned it as heretical, and anathematized those who dared maintain it.

knew very well, I should terribly incommode the Papists. But I find I am caught without hopes of escaping, for the text of the gospel is so clear, as not to be susceptible of misconstruction.'*

* Luther held Christ to be really present together with the bread in the sacrament, as iron and fire are united in a red-hot bar. This sort of presence is called consubstantiation, and is surely as incomprehensible as the Catholic doctrine of transubstantiation. Calvin himself, asserted against Luther, that the doctrine of Catholics was more conformable to Scripture than his. Now, though it is evident that all the difficulties and alleged absurdities, attributed to the Catholic doctrine, equally attach to the Lutheran, yet what preacher has ever attacked the latter, or what civil disabilities has it brought on its followers, while the former has constantly been a subject of profane ridicule for its enemies, and in some countries, for example, Great Britain, a pretext for depriving its followers of their natural rights? This strange difference of conduct must excite the surprise of every reflecting mind. But, as the celebrated statesman, Canning, well observed, in a debate on the Catholic Question, April 21, 1825, 'sympathy is quite the other way;' 'now,' continued he, 'what is it that we object to in the Catholic belief? One doctrine is that of transubstantiation. Yet do we not admit into our religious creed that other doctrine, consubstantiation? which, if any one read Luther's polemic discourse on this subject, he will perceive it to bear so strong an affinity or relationship to the former, as not to be able to ascertain very easily their discrepancy or difference. Yet the opponent to the Catholic claims, will consider the man who professes to believe in consubstantiation, a faithful subject, and denounce the other as a traitor.'

Later Reformers were not so scrupulous, but soon got over the difficulty, by cutting the Gordian knot.

This indeed, is an easy way to get over all the difficulties we meet in the gospel, a way pretty generally followed by the philosophers of the day. But, dear sir, I hope you will not accuse us of superstition for taking a safer way, that of simply believing, even where we cannot understand, how! In believing the real presence of Christ in the eucharist, in believing that we receive the flesh and blood of Christ; in believing that we receive Christ himself, in believing that the substance of the flesh and blood of Christ; so far from being guilty of superstition, we have the satisfaction to know that we believe precisely what Christ commands us to believe, what almost all christendom, these eighteen hundred years, always did believe, and what at present, by far the greatest part of the christian world, above two hundred millions, including the Greek Church, do believe.

I will suppose for a while, sir, that I am wavering, perplexed, uncertain what to believe on the subject of the eucharist, and that I apply to you as a minister of Christ in order to have my doubts resolved, my difficulties removed, and certainty fixed in my mind, what would you tell me, what security could you offer in order to induce me to reject the overwhelming weight of authority which undoubtedly favours the Catholic doctrine of the eucharist, and to persuade me that I ought to believe there is nothing in the sacrament but bread and wine?

You will appeal to my senses, my eyes, my taste, &c. I confess, indeed, sir, that the senses of my body discover nothing in the sacrament but bread and wine, and that I do not see, nor taste the flesh and blood of Christ. But, sir, Christ tells me, 'blessed are they that have not seen and have believed,' John xx. 29.

I would then incline to say with St. Thomas Aquinas

Visus, tactus, gustus in te fallitur
Sed auditu solo tuto creditur
Credo quid quid dixit Dei filius
Nil hoc Verbo veritatis verius.

With nearly all christendom for eighteen centuries, I will sooner believe the testimony of my Divine Saviour, than the testimony of my senses; to speak more correctly, I am not obliged to disbelieve the testimony of my senses, for you know, sir, that what we perceive of any thing by our senses, is not the substance of the thing itself, but mere accidents, such as form, colour, taste, size. Now it is very evident that God, to whom nothing is impossible, may very easily change the substance of a thing and yet continue the accidents, or cause it to make upon my senses the same impression which it did before. This is precisely what the Catholics believe of the eucharist.

Good God! shall we say that Christ has no other way to make his words good, and to give us his flesh and blood, than to reach them to us in their natural form or appearance? Humanity shudders at the thought, and common sense naturally suggests the reason why that sacred food of our souls is given us under the form of the most simple food of the body. You will tell me, perhaps, that according to our doctrines, the body of Christ must be present in a great many places at the same time, which is impossible.

In answer to this objection, I refer you to the system of the most celebrated Protestant philosopher, Mr. Leibnitz, who, besides many others. from the most generally acknowledged principles of metaphysics, and from observations made in natural philosophy, clearly shews that this seeming mystery, the existence of the same body in many places, cannot be proved impossible. But, sir, admitting it to be impossible for a body in its present corruptible state, can the same be said of a glorified body, which St. Paul calls 'a spiritual body?' Can it be said especially of the glorified body of Christ? Pray, sir, do you know any thing at all about the nature of glorified bodies? I must confess I do not; and whilst we are totally ignorant about the nature of a glorified or spiritual body, it appears to me vain to form any opinion about what is possible or impossible for such a body. When I see the glorified body of Christ passing through a door which was shut, John xx. 19, I am willing to believe, that the same body may be present in thousands and millions of places at once; I am willing to believe that that same body may feed my soul, and yet continue glorious in heaven, if such is the will of God, although I cannot comprehend, far less explain, how it can be.

Archbishop Cranmer owns, that Christ may be in the bread and wine, as also in the doors that were shut. Answer to Gardner & Smith, p. 454.

Melancthon says, 'I would rather die than affirm that Christ's body can be but in one place.'

I am sensible, sir, that human reason once seated on the tribunal to judge of the truth or falsehood of revealed mysteries, and guided only by itself, will find a great many more objections. But, sir, as the raging waves, after having beaten against the majestic rock which rises from the bottom of the sea, return in harmless froth; so likewise will all the weak productions of human reason, when beating against the majestic fabric which Christ has raised.

I beg leave here to quote the testimony of three celebrated Protestant divines in favour of the Catholic doctrine.

"The adoration of the eucharist (says Mr. Thorndike) was the practice of the ancient and true church, before receiving,' Epil. L. iii. c. 30 'And I (says the Protestant Bishop Andrews) with St. Ambrose, adore the flesh of Christ in the mysteries,' Andrews to Bel. ch. 8. 'The external adoration of Christ in the eucharist (says the Protestant Bishop Forbes) is the practice of sounder Protestants, and to deny such adoration is a monstrous error of rigid Protestants.' Forbes de Euchar. L. 2.*

* A striking difference may be observed in the style of Protestant controvertists. Those among them who have been deservedly ranked the first for talents, learning, and good sense, are much more temperate in their language, than others who, in the estimation of the public, fall far short of them in the above qualities. In writers of the latter class, do we so often find such expressions as: 'the dogma of the real presence, is absurd:' 'the adoration of Christ in the sacrament is idolatrous and superstitious.' The example of wiser and better men should make them pause before they indulge in the effusions of rashness or malevolence. Before exposing themselves to the danger of blaspheming that which they know not, first, they should reflect that God can reveal nothing absurd: and, secondly, they should fully and impartially examine the proofs of God's having revealed the dogma which they deride. Were our opponents to proceed thus, they would regard the real presence as an adorable mystery, instead of rejecting it as absurd. For, what greater evidence of its divine revelation can be required than the authority of the Scriptures, the doctrine of the Apostles, the testimony

You will object, perhaps, the following words of Christ: 'It is the spirit that quickeneth, the

of all ages, and the consent of all christian nations until the epoch of the Reformation, and even now, the Protestants alone excepted? Finally, the belief of the church in her origin, and the ages immediately succeeding, when her doctrine is allowed to have been pure, and the impossibility that this dogma, if not divinely revealed, could have obtained so firm and constant belief, render it certain that it must have come from Jesus Christ himself.

The following questions and answers are taken from a German Lutheran Catechism, printed in Chambersburg, in 1815, by Johann Herschberger, for William Warner, bookseller, of Baltimore.

Q. What is the last supper of our Lord Jesus Christ?

A. The last supper of Christ is a holy sacrament, a godly word and sign, in which Christ gives us truly and substantially, with bread and wine, his body and blood, and assures us of the forgiveness of our sins, and life everlasting.

Q. What do you receive, eat, and drink in the holy last supper?

A. With bread and wine, I do eat and drink the true body and the true blood of Jesus Christ, as St. Paul says: 'The chalice which we bless, is it not the communion of the blood of Christ? And the bread which we break, is it not the communion of the body of Christ?' 1 Cor. x. 16.

And again, from the 5th article on the Sacrament of the Altar.

Q. What is the sacrament of the altar?

A. It is the true body and blood of our Lord Jesus Christ in the bread and wine, for us christians to eat and drink, instituted by Christ himself, 1 Cor. x. 16, 17, xi. 23, 29.

In both catechisms, the doctrine of the real presence is evidently implied by the words, taken in their obvious flesh profiteth nothing; the words that I have spoken to you, are spirit and life,' John vi. 64.

St. Augustine, who lived about fourteen hundred years ago, explains these words in his 27th treatise on St. John.

'What means, the flesh profits nothing (says St. Augustine.) It profits nothing as they understood it; for they understood flesh, as it is torn in pieces in a dead body, or sold in the shambles; and not as it is animated by the spirit. Wherefore it is said *the flesh profiteth nothing*, in the same manner as it is said *knowledge puffeth up*,' 1 Cor. viii. 1. 'Must we then fly from knowledge? God forbid. What then means *knowledge puffeth up?* That is, if it be alone without charity; therefore, the Apostle added, *but charity edifieth*. Join therefore charity to knowledge, and knowledge will be profitable, not by itself,

---

sense, as they ought to be, since catechetical instructions, being designed for the young and ignorant, and therefore, adapted to the capacity of such, are naturally supposed to contain the plainest exposition of what is to be believed. It may, at first, appear strange, that Protestants should, in their language, approach so near to Catholic doctrine. The reason of this is, that our doctrine is so conformable to Scripture, that they, though differing from us in sentiments, yet affect to hold nearly the same language as we, in order to avoid the palpable contradiction of their professed rule of following the Scriptures in their plain and literal sense.

but through charity; so here also *the flesh profiteth nothing,* viz: the flesh alone. Let the spirit be joined with the flesh, as charity is to be joined with knowledge, and then it profits much. For if the flesh profiteth nothing, the word (Christ) would not have been made flesh, that he might dwell in us.' So far St. Augustine.

Besides *flesh and blood* is often mentioned in Scripture for the corruption of our nature, as when it is said, 'flesh and blood cannot inherit the kingdom of God,' 1 Cor. xv. 50; and 'flesh and blood hath not revealed it unto thee,' Matt. xvi. 17. And in this sense the flesh profiteth nothing to discover and firmly believe what Christ announces; but it is the spirit and grace of God that quickeneth and giveth life to our souls, by inspiring us with a full assent and obedience to divine revelation. Faith is undoubtedly a gift of heaven, and that we may not be deterred by our corrupted reason and senses from believing divine mysteries, we need the light and assistance of God himself. This our Divine Saviour plainly declares in these words: 'therefore did I say to you, that no man can come to me, unless it be given him by my Father,' John vi. 66. So that the foregoing words the flesh profiteth nothing, rather suppose and confirm the truth of the real presence.

But God forbid that we should say the flesh of Christ profits nothing, this would be a blasphemy, and it is evident, that Christ asserting that flesh profits nothing, did not mean his flesh, for this would be contradicting his own assertion, my 'flesh is meat indeed.'

Our doctrine on the eucharist is further confirmed by the ancient figures or types of that sacrament; they were manifold. I shall notice only three of them, viz: the Paschal Lamb, the Blood of the Testament, and the Manna.

1. The Paschal Lamb. That this was a figure of Christ, the Lamb of God, is acknowledged on all hands. The Paschal Lamb was killed at the going out of the land of Egypt on the journey to the land of promise.

The Lamb of God is killed, and we are delivered from a more than Egyptian darkness, and introduced into the road to the real land of promise.

The Paschal Lamb is eaten, Exod. xii. 8; so likewise must the Lamb of God be eaten to accomplish the figure. The Paschal Lamb had no blemish, Exod. xii. 5; the Lamb of God is pure and immacculate by excellence. The blood of the Paschal Lamb was a sign of salvation, Exod. xii. 13. The blood of the Lamb of God is salvation itself. The sacrament of the eucharist was instituted by our Saviour immediately after eating the Paschal Lamb with his disciples; the figure was then accomplished, and the substance substituted for the figure.

2. That the Blood of the Testament, the blood of victims solemnly sacrificed to God, was a figure of the blood of Christ in the sacrament, appears evident from the words of Christ in administering that sacred blood.

Moses said to the people, 'This is the Blood of the Testament, which God hath enjoined to you,' Exod. xxiv. 8. and Heb. ix. 20.

Jesus Christ said to his disciples, 'This is my Blood of the New Testament,' &c. Matt. xxvi. 26.

3. That Manna was a figure of the sacrament of the flesh and blood of Christ, appears from John vi. 58, 'Your fathers did eat Manna and are dead; he that eateth of this bread shall live for ever.' Likewise from 1 Cor. x. 3.

Manna came from the Lord, Exod. xvi. 15; the holy eucharist is also given by our Lord and Saviour, Matt. xxvi.

Manna was given to the Israelites as their food during the whole time of their journey through the desert until they reached the land of promise.

The holy eucharist is given to us as the spiritual food and nourishment of our souls, during the whole time of our mortal pilgrimage, until we reach the true land of promise, our heavenly home. We cannot believe, dear sir, that the figure is better than the thing it represents; St. Paul tells us on the contrary, that the old law had nothing but a *shadow of good things to come,*

Heb. 10. 'That all *its sacrifices and sacraments were* but *weak and beggarly elements,*' Galat. iv. 9. 'And that it was annulled, by reason of *its weakness and unprofitableness,*' Heb. vii. 18.

Now, sir, if the sacrament of the Lord's supper is nothing but bread and wine, it is evident that the figure (manna) is far better than the thing prefigured; for manna comes from heaven; bread comes from the baker's oven.

Manna had a very pleasant taste, and was in many respects miraculous; our bread is a common and natural food.

I have said enough, I think, to convince you, dear sir, that we are not guilty of superstition in believing as we do, on the subject of the holy eucharist, and that our belief on that subject is founded on the plainest words of divine revelation, and not contradicted by reason: add to this, that it is supported by the greatest authority on earth.

Admitting for a while, that the words of Christ were not very plain, or were susceptible of different interpretations, where are we to apply in order to know with certainty the true sense of the words? Are we to adopt the sentiments of any of the Reformers? If so, which are we to select for our guide? Luther held that the bread is the body of Christ; Osiander, that the bread is one and the same person with Christ; Calvin,

Zuinglius, &c. that it is only a figure of the body of Christ. Nay, so far did this diversity of opinions go, that after little more than half a century from the commencement of the Reformation, controvertists counted not less than two hundred different interpretations of the words, 'this is my body.' The numerous sects of the present day, are not less at variance with one another, with respect to this point. What other effect then can such contrariety of belief have, than to bring more strongly to our recollection that observation of Tertullian—'It is natural for error to be ever changing.' But Christ tells us to apply to the church which he has provided with the unerring light of truth for ever. This holy church commands us to believe that in the eucharist, as given by Christ at the last supper, and as consecrated since by legally ordained ministers, are really contained the flesh and blood, the soul and divinity of Jesus Christ—Christ, God and man, Council of Trent, de Euchar. Sacram. Sess. 13, c. 1, 2.

The words used by the confession of Augsburgh seem to convey the very same idea. 'The true body and blood of Jesus Christ are truly present under the form of bread and wine in the Lord's supper, and are there given and received.'

Were we to judge from the approved catechisms of several Protestant sects, they would seem to hold the same doctrine. The church of England in her catechism, declares that, 'the body and blood of Christ are *verily* and *indeed* taken and received by the faithful in the Lord's supper.'

A seemingly weighty objection against the real presence of Christ in the eucharist is found in the following words of our Saviour: 'do this for a commemoration of me,' Luc. xxii. 19; and in the words of St. Paul, 'as often as you shall eat, &c. and drink, &c. you shall shew the death of the Lord until he come,' 1 Cor. xi. 26.

We do not understand how those words can be considered as excluding the real presence of Christ. Whilst man is in his present state of imperfection, carnal, weak, under the influence of his senses, of his imagination, and of so many passions, he is very apt, even whilst engaged in the most solemn of all duties, saying his prayers, or celebrating the divine mysteries, to forget himself, and to perform those duties, through habit, mechanically, and of course, without benefit to himself.

Christ, the subject of our adoration, not being visible in the eucharist, our attention may be very easily diverted from him by objects affecting our senses or imaginations, &c. at the very time we celebrate those mysteries. In order to guard us against that misfortune, we are particularly commanded to direct our attention to our Divine Saviour, to his death upon the cross; we are not to receive his flesh and blood mechanically, but, whilst we receive them, to remember the infinite love of Jesus Christ in immolating that sacred flesh and blood for our salvation, and in feeding our souls with the same.

The command then to remember the death of Christ when we celebrate and receive the Lord's supper so far from excluding the real presence of Christ, is rather founded upon it.

Having now explained to you, dear sir, the doctrine of the Catholic Church concerning the blessed eucharist, this leads me naturally to the explanation of the sacrifice of the mass.

ARTICLE IV.

THE SACRIFICE OF THE MASS.

It is in the mass the holy eucharist is consecrated. The main objection against this sacrifice is its being considered a second sacrifice, whereas it is acknowledged by all christians that the sacrifice of the cross, in which Jesus Christ immolated himself for the salvation of our souls, is the only sacrifice of the new law, and a very sufficient one, as by it, and by it alone, the redemption of man was consummated and God's justice satisfied.

The objection arises from a misunderstanding

The mass so far from being a second sacrifice is only a continuation, and at the same time, a commemoration, of the great sacrifice of the cross.

'Do this in commemoration of me,' says Christ at the last supper to his Apostles, and, of course, to their successors. It is in the mass, dear sir, that this precept of Christ is fulfilled, it is there the bread and wine are consecrated, and by consecration, changed into the body and blood of Christ. In this consecration the blood is mystically separated from the body, as Jesus Christ did separately consecrate the bread into his body, and the wine into his blood, which includes a striking representation and commemoration of that real and violent separation, which took place upon the cross.

By this consecration, as I have shown before, Jesus Christ becomes really present upon the altar, under those signs or forms, which represent his death.

Now Jesus Christ being present in the eucharist, by virtue of the consecration which he himself appointed, 'presents himself, (says St. Paul,) and appears for us, before the face of God,' Heb. ix. 24. Here then is a continuation of the great sacrifice of the cross; here Jesus Christ continues to present to his heavenly Father the merits of his passion and death; he perpetuates the memory of his obedience, even to the death of the cross.

which includes an acknowledgment of God's supreme dominion; of course here is a true and real sacrifice, and yet not a second sacrifice, but only a continuation of the great sacrifice of the cross. Thus the prophecy of Malachias is fulfilled; 'for from the rising of the sun, even to the going down, my name is great among the Gentiles: and in every place there is sacrifice, and there is offered to my name a clean oblation,' &c. Malach. i. 11.

The sacrifice here alluded to cannot be that offered on Mount Calvary on the cross, as that was only offered in one place, of course, it must be the holy sacrifice of the mass; because this is offered in almost every part of the globe, and because Jesus Christ, who there perpetuates the memory of his passion and death, is the only one that can offer a clean oblation to God.

When we consider what Jesus Christ operates in this mystery; when by faith we behold him actually present with these signs of death, we unite ourselves to him in this state; we offer him to God as our only victim, and as the only one, who, by his blood, can merit for us mercy; protesting, at the same time, that we have nothing to offer up to God but Jesus Christ, and the infinite merits of his death. We consecrate all our prayers by this sacred offering, and, in presenting Jesus Christ to God, we are taught to offer up ourselves also in him and by him to his Divine Majesty, as so many living victims. Pray, dear sir, does this doctrine savour of superstition.

Here then is the great sacrifice of christians, differing widely from that, which was in use in the old law, a spiritual sacrifice, and worthy the new covenant; where the victim, though present, is perceptible only by faith; where the immolating sword is the word, which mystically separates the body from the blood; where the shedding of the blood is of course but mystical, and where death intervenes but in representation: a most real sacrifice, however, inasmuch as Jesus Christ is truly contained in it, and presented to his Father under these symbols of death. But still a sacrifice of commemoration, which, far from withdrawing us, as is objected, from the sacrifice of the cross, attaches us to it, by all its circumstances, since the former is not only totally referred to the latter, but in fact has no existence, except by this relation, from which its efficacy is entirely derived.

Such is the express doctrine of the Council of Trent, which teaches that this sacrifice was instituted only 'to represent that which was once offered upon the cross; to perpetuate the memory of it to the end of time; and to apply its saving virtue to us, for the remission of those sins which we every day commit,' Sess. 22, c. 1. The church, then, far from believing the sacrifice of the cross to be by any means defective, is, on the contrary, so convinced of its perfection, that it looks upon every thing done in consequence, as intended merely to commemorate it, and apply its virtue.

We believe then, the holy sacrifice of the mass to be the greatest act of religion that can be performed, the only one perfectly worthy of God, as in that sacrifice Jesus Christ, equal to his Father, is both the high priest and the victim: he is the high priest, inasmuch as he immolates and offers up the victim, which is himself, to his Eternal Father, 'he is the high priest for ever according to the order of Melchisedech,' Ps. cix. 4.

For ever, because although he immolated himself but once in a bloody manner, yet in the mass he perpetuates this sacrifice day after day in an unbloody and mystical manner. *According to the order of Melchisedech*, because 'as Melchisedech brought forth bread and wine, for he was the priest of the most high God,' Gen. xiv. 18. So does Christ the high priest of the new covenant bring forth bread and wine, and having by his omnipotence changed them into his flesh and blood, continues under those forms of bread and wine to offer himself up, to present to his heavenly Father the merits of his passion and death, and likewise under these forms to feed and nourish the souls of men.

Whoever is in the least versed in the history of the church and the writings of the holy fathers, will readily acknowledge, that the mass was always considered as the great sacrifice of the new covenant, and that the practice of celebrating mass is as ancient as christianity.

In all the liturgies of the ancient churches, we trace the words, sacrifice, immolation, altar, priesthood, host, victim, namely Christ really present; and consequently, all the conditions of a true and perfect sacrifice. Now, the liturgies exhibit to us the belief of the whole church, even in the first ages, since they are themselves very ancient. They are ascribed to St. James, St. Mark, St. Basil, and St. Chrysostom, and have been carefully preserved, not only by the Latins and Greeks, but also by the Nestorians, Eutychians, &c. who departed from the church 1400 years ago.

It is the same with the holy fathers. St. Irenaus, bishop of Lyons, in the second century, says: 'Christ took that which is naturally bread, and gave thanks, saying, this is my body; and he taught the new oblation of the new covenant, which the church receiving from the Apostles, every where presents to God. This Malachias had foretold,' &c. Ad. Haer. lib. iv. cap. 23. In the third century, St. Cyprian, bishop of Carthage, says: 'who is the priest of the Most High in a more perfect manner, than our Lord, who offered a sacrifice to God, and offered the same that had been offered by Melchisedech, namely, bread and wine, that is, his body and blood?' Epist. 68 ad Caecilium.

In the fourth century, St. Cyril of Jerusalem, says: 'when we offer the sacrifice, we pray for our departed brethren; believing that their souls receive much assistance from the awful sacrifice of our altars,' Catech. 5.

St. Chrysostom, bishop of Constantinople, says: 'the wise men worshipped him in the manger, thou seest him not in the manger, but on the altar,' &c. in 1 Cor.

Again, 'from its being offered in many places, are there then many Christs?' No: for as he who is every where offered is one body, and not many bodies, so the sacrifice is one, Hom. 17, in Hebr. In the same age, St. Ambrose says: 'when we sacrifice, Christ is present,' in Cap. 1 Luc.

St. Augustine of the fifth age, says: 'when now we see this sacrifice offered to God in every place by the priesthood of Christ, according to the order of Melchisedech, and the Jews' sacrifice cease, why do 'they yet expect another Christ?'' De Civitate Dei, c. 35. And in book ix. of his Confessions, c. 3, he tells us, his mother Monica desired on her death-bed, to be remembered at the altar, where she knew the holy sacrifice to be offered, wherewith the indictment against us was blotted out.

In another place he says: 'Christ is at the same time both the priest that offers, and the host (or victim) which is offered; and he would that the sacrifice which the church daily offers, should be the sacrament and the representation of this mystery; because the church being the body of that Divine Head, it offers itself by him.' All these holy fathers and bishops of the church lived some 1100, some 1200 years before the pretended Reformation; at a time when even the most learned Protestants own that the church of Christ had not yet gone astray. In the sixth age, that is, about 1000 years before the Reformation, St. Gregory the Great, by whose means England was converted, has the following remarkable words, in a sermon which he preached on Christmas day: 'whereas by the grace of God, we shall this day celebrate mass three times, we cannot speak very long on the gospel,' Homil. 8. in Evangel.

Such was the practice of the church 1300 years ago, and such is the practice of the church at present in 1815;* on Christmas day every priest celebrates mass three times.

If then, dear sir, we are guilty of superstition in celebrating mass, and believing as we do of the mass, it is a great comfort to us to find, that our superstition is no other than that, of which were guilty all the holiest and wisest bishops of the

* Now 1841

most remote antiquity. It is a great comfort to us to know, that the church had already existed more than 1500 years before it was found out, that to celebrate mass and to believe that Christ is really present in the eucharist, are superstitious practices and doctrines.

Before I conclude this important subject, I should not omit explaining the practice of the Catholic Church of giving communion under one kind or form.

ARTICLE V.

COMMUNION UNDER ONE KIND OR FORM.

Upon this head we are accused of depriving the laity of an essential part of the sacrament.

From the moment, dear sir, the real presence of Christ in the eucharist is admitted, there can exist no difference on this subject. It must be a matter of perfect indifference whether we receive the holy communion under one or both kinds.*

---

* If the precept of Christ, drink ye all of this, regard not the Apostles only, who alone were present, and were then ordained priests, for offering, under both kinds, this holy sacrifice, which was to be continued by their lawful successors, but be extended to all persons indifferently, the absurd consequence will be, that all are priests

'Christ rising from the dead,' says St. Paul, 'dieth no more,' Rom. vi. 9. Consequently wherever Christ is, there also is Christ's body; wherever the flesh of Christ is, there also is his blood, his soul and divinity; and where his blood is, there is also his flesh, &c. To say that Christ is divided between the two kinds or forms, so as for one form to contain the one-half, and for the other form to contain the other half of Christ, would be impious. But it is said, that in giving communion under one kind, and depriving lay people of the chalice, we transgress the commandment of Christ, who, at the last supper said, 'drink ye all of this,' &c. &c.

In answer to this, we say, that Christ only

Moreover, did we Catholics hold the mere figurative system, we could not deny that there would be some reason for receiving the liquid as well as the solid substance, as the former may appear to represent more aptly the blood, and the latter the body. But believing as we do, Christ to be really present, we believe that he is equally and entirely present under each species, and consequently, is equally and entirely given to the faithful, whichever they receive. The Catholic clergy, far from thinking that they wrong the laity by withholding the cup, always act conformably to this belief. Hence, when any of them are prevented by corporal infirmity, or any other cause, from offering the holy sacrifice, and wish to communicate, they receive under one kind. The same is observed at the hour of death, when the viaticum is always administered under one kind to the clergy as well as to the laity.

spoke to his Apostles, as it is certain that none were present at the last supper but they. The precept then was directed to the Apostles, in obedience to which they and their successors to this day, when they celebrate the holy mysteries, always receive under both kinds.

St. Paul very clearly states that communion may be validly received under either kind alone; 'Wherefore, whosoever shall eat this bread, *or* drink the chalice of the Lord unworthily,' &c. 1 Cor. xi. 27. I know, dear sir, that your Protestant translations say eat *and* drink, instead of eat *or* drink; but if you compare the Catholic translation with the genuine original Greek, you will find it correct. The sufficiency of one kind in the holy communion is clearly acknowledged by the Calvinists of France in two of their synods. The Synod of Poiters, held A. D. 1560, has the following words:

'The bread of the Lord's supper ought to be administered to those who cannot drink wine, upon their making a protestation that it is not out of contempt, when they also obviate all scandal by bringing the cup as near to their mouth as they possibly can,' Synod of Poiters, chap. 12, article 7th of the Lord's supper.

The same was again approved and confirmed by the Synod of La Rochelle, A. D. 1571.

After all I have said, dear sir, you will conceive that Catholics are not guilty of superstition in believing as they do on the subject of the Lord's supper and the mass.

They are compelled to believe so by the combined weight of heavenly and earthly authority, which overrules the dictates and judgment of our corrupted senses, and of our weak and limited reason; and to all the arguments of human reason, or if you choose, philosophy, we answer with St. Paul, 'Our faith does not stand on the wisdom of man, but on the power of God,' 1 Cor. ii. 5.

I must confess that I am less surprised to see a person (with the Socinians) rejecting all mysteries, than to see him admit one and reject another, though the latter is perhaps more clearly expressed in the written word than the former.

Although I detest the impiety of the Socinian, yet I cannot but acknowledge his consistency, and should I ever have the misfortune (which God in his tender mercy forbid) to forsake the unerring guide, which now overawes and silences my reason into perfect submission, and should I ever become so much blinded by a more than diabolical pride, as to make my limited and corrupted reason the sole arbiter of my faith, I think it would suggest to me the rejection of all mysteries, of every thing incomprehensible to that reason, and thus lead me at once into the paths of Socinianism. The same reason that would suggest to me the absurdity of eating the flesh of Christ, would likewise suggest the absurdity of three distinct persons in the divinity, which is essentially one.

If you cast your eyes around you, (without traveling many miles from home,) do you not see, in many respectable members of society, the deplorable consequences of trusting to the light of reason, and refusing submission to unerring authority? Do you not perceive in many of those, whose reason has been developed by a liberal education, a perfect indifference, (if not a kind of contempt,) for the mysteries in general, and even in particular for those very mysteries which by all societies are considered the fundamental principles of christianity? In proportion as the powers of their understanding have been improved, they seem to have acquired a greater right to set up their reason as a judge over the divine mysteries, and thus to abuse the noblest gift of God to purposes of impiety.

The whole system of the christian religion; the greatest of all the works of God, one and indivisible, must be believed in the whole and in all its parts; neither does it require less impiety to reject one part of that divine system known to be revealed by Jesus Christ, than to reject the whole. Now, sir, from what you see, I mean the rejection both in principle and practice, of so many mysteries among Protestants, and this is only a natural consequence of making limited reason the arbiter of faith; how long, do you suppose, will it be until faith will be entirely extinct? Will the present generation of children, after coming to the age of maturity, remember that their parents were christians? Will the next generation even enjoy the benefit of baptism? I am acquainted with many youths of both sexes, who, although born of Protestant parents, never received the benefit of baptism. Why so? Because their Protestant parents, guided by the light of reason, could not see into the necessity of baptism, and thus probably judged it an idle ceremony. Thus is the child's eternal fate left to rest on the private opinions of their parents on religious mysteries, as if our merciful God had left us in a state of uncertainty, in those matters principally, in which certainty is absolutely necessary.

After this digression, which a sincere zeal for the salvation of souls has occasioned, I shall continue to explain a few remaining articles of Catholic faith. Having explained the Catholic doctrine of the mass, this leads me to the Catholic doctrine of purgatory and prayers for the dead.

ARTICLE VI.

PURGATORY AND PRAYERS FOR THE DEAD

WHAT has induced the gentlemen of the pretended Reformation, to discard purgatory from their creed, and to renounce the practice of praying for the deceased, I am at a loss to know. To any man of information, it must be notorious, that the belief and the practice are older than christianity, almost universal, and far from being impervious to human reason, must, upon a candid examination, meet the approbation of reason.

The Catholic Church, the supreme tribunal of our faith, teaches that 'there is a purgatory, a place of temporal punishment after death, and that the souls therein detained are helped by the prayers of the faithful, and especially by the holy sacrifice of the mass,' Concil. Trident. Sess. 25, Decret. de Purg. This decree of the church, assembled in general council, is sufficient for a Catholic to regulate his faith on the present subject, and to convince him fully of the existence of a purgatory, and of the usefulness of prayers for the dead. Still it is a satisfaction to a Catholic, already convinced by the authority of the church, to find that even the plain words of Scripture, and the plainest dictates of reason, are in perfect unison with the declaration of the church Long before the coming of Christ, the people of God prayed and offered sacrifice for the dead. Witness the collection of money made by Judas Macchabæus, the defender of God's sanctuary; 'and making a gathering, he sent twelve thousand drachms of silver to Jerusalem for sacrifice to be offered for the sins of the dead, thinking well and religiously concerning the resurrection—it is therefore a holy and wholesome thought to pray for the dead, that they may be loosed from sins,' 2 Maccab. xii. 43—46. I know that Protestants reject the Macchabees. But you will permit me to observe that this rejection, made by modern Reformers, can bear no weight, when made in opposition to all antiquity, in opposition to the universal church, the only one extant at the time of the pretended Reformation.

In the earliest ages of christianity we find the holy fathers quoting the Macchabees, as well as other Scriptures. Witness St. Clement of Alexandria, *lib.* 6, *Stromat.*; *Origen, lib.* 2, *de Principiis, cap.* 1; *St. Cyprian, lib. de Exhortatione Martyrii*; *St. Jerom, cap.* 23; *Isai.*; *St. Augustine, lib.* 8, *de Civitate Dei, cap.* 36. *St. Isidore Hispalensis* says, 'the Books of the Macchabees, although separated by the Hebrews as Apocrypha, are by the church of Christ honoured, and proclaimed as Divine books,' *lib.* 6. The General

Council of Trent, Sess. 4, declares the two Macchabees to be Divine books.*

The belief of a middle state is supported by many other texts of the Old and New Testaments.

'Thou also by the blood of thy testament, has sent forth thy prisoners out of the pit, wherein is no water,' Zach. ix. 11.

That pit cannot be hell, as out of hell there is

---

* The Council of Trent, in defining the Divine Inspiration of those books, has only followed the constant and unanimous tradition of the church, and the examples of other councils, some of which were even general. For those books had been reckoned among the sacred writings by the General Council of Florence, held in 1439, under Eugenius IV.; by a council of seventy bishops, held in Rome in 494, under Pope Gelasius; by Pope St. Innocent I. in his famous epistles, written in 405, to St. Exuperius, bishop of Tholouse; by the third Council of Carthage, held in 397, at which St. Augustin assisted; by St. Augustin himself, in his work on Christian Doctrine, book xxii. chap. 28, and in the City of God, book xviii. chap 36; in a word, by many other fathers.

The Books of Macchabees must be allowed, even by those who do not receive them as canonical, to be, at least, authentic records; as such, then, they bear undeniable testimony of the belief and practice of the Jews of the present day, who, surely, have not borrowed them from Catholics. Seeing, then, the doctrine of purgatory and praying for the dead to have been held by God's people 150 years before Christ, what are we to think of the candour of those who assert it to be an invention of the dark ages?

no redemption. Consequently it must be a place of temporal punishment from which redemption is had by the blood of the testament.

'Every man's work shall be made manifest: for the Lord shall be revealed by fire: and the fire shall try every man's work, of what sort it is. If any man's work abide, which he has built thereupon, he shall receive a reward. If any man's work burn, he shall suffer loss: but he himself shall be saved, yet so as by fire,' 1 Cor. iii. 13. 14. 15.

This text hardly requires any comment. From it appears plainly, that although the works of man have been substantially good, and pleasing to Almighty God, yet on account of many deformities, the effects of human frailty and corruption, man must be cleansed by a purging and punishing, yet saving fire, before he can be admitted into that sanctuary; into which 'nothing defiled can enter,' Apocalypse xxi. 27. 'But I say unto you, that every idle word that men shall speak, they shall render an account for it, in the day of judgment,' Matt. xii. 36. Dear sir, you will hardly say that every idle word will consign man to the everlasting punishments of hell! If so, who will be saved? There must then be some temporal punishments prepared after this life for trifling faults, which we call venial sins.

According to the same Evangelist there are sins that 'shall not be forgiven neither in this world nor in the world to come,' Matt. xii. 32. Does not this intimate that some sins may be atoned for in the world to come?

'Make an agreement with thy adversary quickly, whilst thou art in the way with him: lest perhaps the adversary deliver thee to the judge, and the judge deliver thee to the officer, and thou be cast into prison. Amen I say to thee, thou shalt not go out from thence, until thou pay the last farthing,' Matt. v. 25, 26.

The last text I am going to quote, establishes the doctrine of a third place so very plainly, that it appears strange how it can be misunderstood.

'Christ also died once, for our sins, the just for the unjust, that he might offer us to God, being put to death indeed in the flesh, but brought to life by the spirit, in which also he came and preached to those spirits who were in prison: who in time past had been incredulous, when they waited for the patience of God, in the days of Noe, when the ark was building,' &c. 1 Peter iii. 18, 19, 20.

It will hardly be supposed that Christ preached to the damned spirits in hell, as it is acknowledged on all hands, I believe, that there is no redemption for them. How then can the above text be understood, unless by admitting a place of temporal punishment, in which were confined those, who in the time of Noah, were incredulous, and who had not fully satisfied the justice of God before departing this life.

The doctrine of the existence of a third place is founded on the belief, that very often, after the guilt and the eternal punishment are taken away by the mercy of God, upon the sinner's sincere repentance, there still remains, on account of the defects of that repentance, something due to the infinite justice of God, something to be expiated either in this world or in the next. Nothing indeed can be more clearly established in Scripture.

Adam was cast out of the earthly paradise, himself and all his posterity punished with death and many miseries, after his sin of disobedience had been forgiven, and his right to heaven restored to him.

David was punished with the death of his child, after his enormous crimes were forgiven, after his sincere repentance, 2 Kings c. xii. 'O king,' saith Daniel to Nabuchodonosor, 'redeem thy sins with alms.' Dan. c. iv. 24.

If temporal punishments have often been inflicted by the justice of God, after the guilt and the everlasting punishments were remitted, it follows of course, that if the person die before he has suffered that temporal punishment, he dies that much indebted to God's justice, and must undoubtedly discharge that debt before he can enter into heaven.

The writings of the holy fathers of both the eastern and the western church, most clearly prove that from the earliest dawn of christianity, the belief of a purgatory was general in the church. Tertullian, who lived in the second age, says, 'No man will doubt but that the soul doth recompense something in the places below,' Lib. de Anima c. 58.

And again, in his book de Corona Militis, 'we make yearly oblations for the dead.'

St. Clement in the same age tells us, St. Peter 'taught them, among other works of mercy, to bury the dead, and diligently perform their funeral rites, and also to pray and give alms for them,' Epist. 1, de S. Petro.

In the third age, St. Cyprian says, 'It is one thing to be cast into prison, and not to go out thence till he pay the last farthing; another, presently to receive the reward of faith; one thing to be afflicted with pains for sins to be expiated, and purged long with fire; another, to have purged all sins by sufferings,' Epis. 52, ad Antone. In the same age Origen says, 'though a releasement out of prison be promised,' St. Matt. v, 'yet it is signified, that none can get out from thence, but he who pays the last farthing.' In Epist. ad Roman, and Hom. 35, in St. Luc.

In the fourth age, St. Ambrose, 'But whereas St. Paul says, *yet so as by fire,* he shows indeed that he shall be saved, but yet shall suffer the punishment of fire, he may be saved, and not tormented for ever, as the infidels are with everlasting fire.' Cap. 3, Epis. ad Cor.

In the same age, 'this is that (says St. Jerome) which he saith, thou shalt not go out of prison, till thou shalt have paid for even thy little sins,' C. v. Matt.

In the same age, St. Cyril of Jerusalem says: 'We beseech God for all those who have died before us, believing the obsecration of that holy and dreadful sacrifice, which is put on the altar, to be the greatest help of the souls for which it is offered,' Catech. Mystagog. 5.

Again, in the same age, St. John Chrysostom, says, 'these things were not in vain ordained by the Apostles, that in the venerable and dreadful mysteries, the mass, there should be made a memory of those who have departed this life; they knew much benefit would hence accrue to them.' Homil. 3, in Epist. ad Philip. It would fill volumes to quote all those passages from the holy fathers which prove the belief in a third place, and prayers for the dead, to be coeval with christianity. Those whom I have quoted lived twelve, thirteen and fourteen centuries before the pretended Reformation, and were of course better judges of genuine apostolical tradition than the late Reformers could be.

If these holy and learned doctors, some of whom were the immediate successors of the Apostles, did not think themselves guilty of superstition in praying for the dead, but declared that in doing so, they followed and obeyed the ordinances of the Apostles; neither are we guilty of superstition in believing and doing as they did.

An objection against purgatory is found in the following words of Scripture: 'If the tree fall to the south, or to the north, in what place soever it shall fall, there it shall be,' Eccles. xi. 3.

Admitting that the Scripture here speaks of the soul after death, which indeed is highly probable, how does this make against purgatory?

We believe, that there are only two eternal states after death, *viz.* the state of glory and the state of damnation. If the soul departs in the state of grace, it shall be for ever in that state, although it may have some venial sins to satisfy for, which may for a while retard the consummation of its happiness. If it dies in the state of mortal sin, and an enemy of God, it shall be ever in torments. Here are two everlasting states, which may be meant by the north and south of the above text. This is the interpretation of St. Jerome, St. Gregory Pope, St. Bernard, St. Thomas, &c. It is besides so satisfactory that it is surprising that Protestants, instead of admitting it, vainly endeavour to discover in the text the nonexistence of purgatory. How any one can see in it the exclusion of our doctrine, I cannot conceive.

I shall now undertake to prove, that the belief in a place of temporal punishment, after death, far from being unreasonable, is perfectly agreeable to the dictates of sound reason, and here I shall borrow the words of the Philosophical Catechism, Art. vii. sect. 4, N. 480.

'Here is what a christian orator and philosopher might say: the soul of man ceasing to dwell upon earth, is summoned to appear before the tribunal of God; his works and virtues speak for him; the law, which he has religiously observed, stands up in his defence to get him crowned in the assembly of the saints. A slight transgression, a foible hardly perceptible, a small failing, inseparable from mortal nature, is perceived in a crowd of meritorious deeds. You, who acknowledge a just God, who adore a merciful God, and yet a God inimical to all iniquity, incapable by nature of admitting into his abode any thing sullied with guilt: say, what is to be the fate of this soul, righteous indeed, though stained with sin; a friend to God, yet bearing in its bosom an enemy to God? Shall its sins be placed along with its virtues? Its weakness and its fortitude be crowned alike? Its christian works confounded with the works of natural frailty? No, you will never think it; nor have even the adversaries of the tenet of purgatory ever ventured to say it openly. But, must this unfortunate soul be eternally reproved without mercy or resource? Shall the purity of its faith, the liveliness of its hope, the good works without number or measure it has performed, plead for it in vain? Far be it from us to think it. By thinking so, we should attack the infinite excellence and perfections of the sovereign Lord of this world. No; never will God rank in the same category, inadvertence and malice, a distraction in prayer and the total neglect of it, an officious lie and a detestable perjury, the man with a few blemishes, and the miscreant sunk over head and ears in profligacy; he will purify the one and reprobate the other; he is at once the God of all justice, and the God of all sanctity. A holy soul, but sullied by a stain, shall not enter his mansion, because he is the God of sanctity, and yet shall enter, because he is the God of justice. He, therefore, will reform it, will complete the lustre of its virtues, establish the purity of its works, and then will place it in his glory.' There is the solid foundation of the belief of a purgatory, and such is the conclusion we are to draw from the incontestable attributes of our Judge and our God. Hence it is that of all the tenets of the Catholic Church, the most widely diffused, and the most generally admitted, is the tenet of purgatory. The knowledge of a God, both just and holy, has united the most inimical religions, and the most opposite to one another, in the belief of a purgatory, that is, of a certain delay put to the eternal reward, during which the just man is still more sanctified; an offended God does not damn, for venial sins, because his wrath does not extend to the offender's death, nor a remunerating God confer his rewards immediately, because his liberality is restrained by the faults of a just yet guilty man. This the sages of antiquity have taught in their books, Plato and Timæo; this the profane, but sublime, poets have sung in their hymns, Virgil's Ænedi, L. vi. v. 730; this the nations, misled by Mahomet, profess in their Alcoran; in this the Hebrews, both ancient and modern, agree with the christians; and the Greeks, severed from the church by a long and obstinate schism, pray for the dead.

Here then is the greatest part of mankind, all that believe in revelation, except those who follow our late Reformers, and numbers of those wh are guided by reason alone, agreed in the belie of a place of temporal punishment, and in th practice of praying for the dead.

If then the Protestant continues to assert th. he cannot find either purgatory or the practice of praying for the dead in Scripture, the Catholic Church answer, that they find both the doctrine and the practice very clearly in Holy Scripture

If the Protestant peremptorily decides, that the belief in purgatory is absurd, and the practice of praying for the dead ridiculous, we, in our sober senses, possessed of common sense as well as our good Protestant neighbours, enlightened by a liberal education as well as many of them, endowed with genius and talents, capable of the most profound disquisitions, in short, endowed, many of us, with all the perfections of the understanding which nature can give, or education improve, we answer, that we find the belief in a place of temporal punishment, and the practice of praying for the dead, perfectly reasonable.

Here then is reason opposed to reason, common sense to common sense, genius and talents to genius and talents; the reason, common sense, &c. of very many in favour of purgatory opposed to the reason, common sense, &c. of comparatively few against purgatory.

Who shall decide, and decide so as to put the question for ever to rest? None but the great tribunal which Jesus Christ established on earth more than eighteen hundred years ago. When infusing into his ministers the spirit of truth, he promised that that spirit should never depart from them to the end of time. This tribunal, as I have proved above, has decided in our favour, and it is because that supreme and infallible tribunal has decided so, that we believe as we do.

Just as I was going to close the present subject, a little pamphlet fell into my hands, the author of which calls himself an independent minister, in which I find the following objection against purgatory

'This doctrine of purgatory casts a reproach on Christ as a Saviour of sinners, representing his obedience and suffering as insufficient to atone for their sins.'

This objection, dear sir, will appear very trifling to you when you know, that the Catholic Church teaches, that the merits of Jesus Christ are of themselves far more than sufficient to atone for all the sins of mankind. But Jesus Christ requires our co-operation; and it depends upon the degree of our co-operation, whether those infinite merits of Christ are applied to us in a more or less abundant measure.

It is in the order of grace as in the order of nature, 'In the sweat of thy face, shalt thou eat bread,' Gen. iii. 19.

God's omnipotence alone gives growth to our grain; yet without casting a reproach on that omnipotence we may safely assert, that, *cæteris paribus*, in proportion as we plough and sow, in that proportion we shall reap. So, likewise, although Christ's merits and satisfaction for sinners are of infinite value, yet the benefit we shall reap of those infinite merits will be proportionate to our endeavours in subduing our corrupt nature, our sinful inclinations, and conforming to the will of God.

'He who soweth sparingly shall reap sparingly; and he who soweth in blessing shall also reap of blessings,' 2 Cor. ix. 6.

He, then, who soweth so sparingly in this world as to remain, in his dying moment, indebted to the Divine Justice, will, after his death, be compelled to pay to the last farthing what, by more strenuous endeavours, he might have paid in this world.

I believe, sir, I have fulfilled my promise of proving, that we are not guilty of superstition in believing a purgatory, and praying for the dead. I shall now try to prove, that we are no more guilty of superstition in honouring the saints, and applying to their intercession.

ARTICLE VII.

HONOURING THE SAINTS, AND APPLYING TO THEIR INTERCESSION.

Few of the tenets of our holy religion are attacked with more virulence, than the present one; but pray, sir, how is it attacked? By misrepresentation; it is exhibited in a most odious form, and then this phantom, the offspring of a heated imagination, or perhaps of a malicious heart, is attacked by the most violent abuse, the very worst of bad arguments; it is attacked with the powerful arms of ridicule and low ribaldry.

According to the bold assertions delivered from Protestant pulpits, and propagated from Protestant presses, we worship the saints, we make gods of them, we consider them as our mediators, we give them the honour belonging to God alone, &c.

The General Council of Trent expressly teaches, that 'the saints who reign with Christ offer up their prayers to God for men, and that it is good and useful to invoke them, and in order to obtain from God, blessings through his son Jesus Christ our Lord, *who alone is our Redeemer and Saviour,* to have recourse to their prayers, help and assistance,' Conc. Trid. Sess. 25. Again,

'Although the church does sometimes offer up masses in honour and in memory of the saints, yet it is not to them, but to God alone, who has crowned them, that the sacrifice is offered up: therefore, the priest does not say, I offer up this sacrifice to thee, Peter, or thee, Paul, but to God himself, giving thanks to him for their victories, imploring their patronage, that they may vouchsafe to intercede for us in heaven, whose memory we celebrate on earth,' Con. Trid. Sess. 25, c. 2.

You will readily acknowledge, dear sir, that there is a wide difference between divine worship and simple honour or reverence. Divine worship belongs to God alone, honour and reverence may be paid to many of God's creatures. Thus, even by God's commandment, we honour our parents, our superiors in church and state, we honour persons respectable for their rank, dignity, virtue, talents, &c. and all this without robbing God of that honour and reverence justly due to him.

If then, it is no sin to honour poor mortals who are yet in this place of trial, of whose eternal fate we are very uncertain, why should it be sin to honour those whom the great God has been pleased to honour with a seat of eternal glory in his kingdom. All the power, riches and glory of this world are nothing in comparison to a single ray of glory emanating from the lowest saint in heaven.

What honour does not a monarch receive over the whole earth? And perhaps he is a very great sinner; perhaps a victim of God's eternal vengeance; how much more honour and reverence is even the least saint in heaven entitled to? The Council of Trent ordering sacrifice to be offered to God alone, confines divine worship to God, but at the same time recommends the saints to be remembered and honoured, and their intercession, in our behalf, to be implored.

The catechism of the Council of Trent (part 3) explains the prodigious difference there is between the manner of imploring the assistance of God, and that of imploring the assistance of saints; 'we pray to God,' it says, 'either to grant us good things, or to deliver us from evil: but because the saints are more agreeable to him than we are, we beg of them to plead in our behalf, and to obtain of God for us whatever we stand in need of.' Hence it is, that we make use of two forms of prayer, widely different from one another; for, in speaking to God, we say, *have mercy on us, hear us,* whereas, in addressing ourselves to a saint, we say no more than *pray for us.*

It is a very ancient and common practice among christians to ask one another's prayers, and to pray for one another. 'I beseech you,' says St. Paul, 'that you also help me in your prayers to God for me,' Rom. xv. 30. 'I make my prayer,' says St. John, 'that thou mayest prosper as to all things, and be in health,' &c. 3 John 2.

The holy Apostles then, in applying to the intercession of others, or praying for them, did not think they were guilty of derogating from any of the divine perfections, or of attributing to mere creatures, what belongs to God alone. Neither are we guilty of derogating from the perfections of God, when we apply to one another's intercession. Why then should we be guilty of derogating from the perfections of God, by applying to the intercession of his saints in heaven, admitting that the saints are able to hear our prayers, and willing to offer their intercession in our behalf? You will readily acknowledge, dear sir, that their intercession must be more efficacious than the intercession of our fellow-mortals. If then praying to the saints is by the gentlemen of the Reformation, considered as superstitious, it must be, because the saints are considered too far from us to hear our prayers; or because they are thought unwilling to apply in our behalf. Such, indeed, is the objection I find in a book called the *Morning Exercise against Popery*, which is a collection of sermons preached by twenty-four Protestant ministers, with the avowed purpose of detecting and confuting errors of the Roman Catholic Church. 'This practice is irrational, (says Mr. Mayo, in his sermon against invocation of saints and angels, p. 525,) there is nothing more absurd. Consider (says he) their incapacity to hear the prayers that are directed to them. That this is the case of the glorified spirits is evident, because 1. They are not omnipresent; they are circumscribed and finite creatures, and can be but in one place at once. 2. They are not omnipercipient; if they should hear what men say with their mouths, they cannot perceive or understand what men say in their hearts.' Here is logic indeed!

The saints and angels are not every where, do

not know every thing, therefore they do not hear our prayers, far less perceive our thoughts. Such and no better will be the way of reasoning of any person, who has no other guide than reason blinded by prejudice.

Beginning where he should end, he will lay down as self-evident the very matters in dispute, without any better proof than his own bold and presumptuous assertion, it is certain, it is absurd, it is self-evident, &c. and thus starting from false principles, his conclusion can be no better.

Mr. Mayo, and I suppose all the gentlemen of the Reformation, take it for granted, then, that saints and angels do not hear our prayers, far less perceive our thoughts. Now, sir, abstracting for awhile from the decision of the Catholic Church, which for Catholics is sufficient, and taking the present question on your own ground, what does Scripture say? 'There shall be joy before the angels of God upon one sinner doing penance,' Luc. xv. 10. The angels then see our thoughts.

'Take heed that ye despise not one of these little ones, for I say to you their angels that are in heaven, always see the face of my Father,' Matt. xviii. 10. The angels then know when we are injured, and pray to God in our behalf; and the saints are as 'the angels of God in heaven,' Matt. xxii. 30. 'Equal to the angels,' Luke xx. 36.

'When thou didst pray, said the angel Raphael

to Tobias, I offered thy prayer to the Lord,' Tob xii. 12.

'The angels are all ministering spirits, sent to minister for them who shall receive the inheritance of salvation,' Heb. i. 14. And that God gives the saints great power in the government of this world is plain from the following:

'He that shall overcome, and keep my works to the end, to him will I give power over the nations, and he shall rule them with a rod of iron,' Apoc. ii. 26, 27.

That angels and saints actually pray for us, is likewise plainly stated in Scripture. 'The angel of the Lord answered and said, O Lord of hosts, how long wilt thou not have mercy on Jerusalem, and the cities of Juda, with which thou hast been angry these three score and ten years?' Zach. i. 12. The four and twenty ancients fell down before the Lamb, having every one of them harps, and golden vials full of odours, which are the prayers of the saints, Apoc. v. 8. And Judas Macchabeus saw in a vision Onias that had been high priest, holding up his hands and praying for the Jews, and pointing also to another, in these words: this is a lover of the brethren, who prayeth much for the people and for the holy city namely, Jeremias, the prophet of God, 2 Macchab xv. 12, 13, 14. They had both been dead many years.

That the practice of honouring and praying to the saints, is as ancient as christianity, is evident from the testimony of the holy fathers in all ages. The belief of the first age on this point, will appear from St. Ignatius, who requesting, a little before his martyrdom, which happened in 107, the prayers of the Trallians for himself and his church, adds thus, 'that my soul may intercede for you, not only in this life, but hereafter in the presence of my God.'

St. Justin, the martyr, who lived in the second age, says, we venerate and worship the angelic host, and the spirits of the prophets, teaching others as we ourselves have been taught.

'I will begin to fall down on my knees,' says the learned Origen, who lived in the third age, 'and pray to all the saints to succour me, who dare not ask God, for the exceeding greatness of my sin. O saints of God! with tears and weeping I beseech you to fall down before his mercy for me a wretch,' in Lament.

And again, 'all the saints departed, still bearing charity towards the living, it will not be improper to say, that they have a care of their salvation, and help them with their prayers to God for them, &c. Homil. 3, in Cant.

St. Ambrose, who lived in the fourth age, says: 'that my prayer may be more efficacious, I call upon the intercession of the B. V. Mary, I ask the prayers of the Apostles, the assistance of the martyrs and confessors,' Prep. for Death. And, again, it is our duty to pray to the angels who have been given us to be our guardians. We should address our prayers to the martyrs, whose bodies still remaining among us, are pledges of their protection. Neither let us blush to ask their intercession under our infirmities, since they, even when they conquered, knew what infirmities are.

In the same age lived St. Basil, who expressly refers this practice to the Apostles, where he says, 'I invoke the Apostles, Prophets, and Martyrs to pray for me, that God may be merciful to me, and forgive me my sins, since this has been ordained by tradition from the Apostles, and is practiced in all our churches.'

In the fifth age, St. Augustin says, 'we do not pray for the holy martyrs, but we recommend ourselves to their prayers,' Tract. 84, in Joan.

Instead of quoting any more of the holy fathers, I cannot forbear giving you here the opinion of the learned Protestant Bishop Montague on this subject.

'I do not deny,' says he, 'but the saints are mediators, as they are called, of prayer and intercession, but in general, and for all in general. They interpose with God by their supplications and mediate by their prayers,' Antid. p. 20. The same Bishop Montague owns that the blessed in heaven do recommend to God in their prayers their kindred, friends and acquaintances on earth; and having given his reason, he says, 'this common voice with general concurrence, without contradiction of reverend and learned antiquity, for aught I ever could read or understand; and I see no cause or reason to dissent from them touching intercession, in this kind,' Treat. Invoc. of Saints. p. 103. He owns also that it is no injury to the mediation of Christ, to ask of the saints to pray for us. 'Indeed I grant Christ is not wronged in his mediation; it is no impiety to say, as they of the Roman Church do, holy Mary pray for me; holy Peter pray for me,' p. 118. And again, 'I see no absurdity in nature, no incongruity unto analogy of faith, no repugnancy at all to sacred Scripture, much less, impiety, for any man to say, holy angel guardian pray for me.'

It is true, the same Protestant Bishop seems in another place to express a doubt whether the saints can hear or know our prayers.

'Could I come at them,' he says, 'or certainly inform them of my state, without any question or much ado, I would readily and willingly say, holy Peter, blessed Paul, pray for me; recommend my case unto Christ Jesus our Lord. Were they with me, by me in my kenning, I would run with open arms and fall upon my knees, and with affection, desire them to pray for me.'

The only difficulty then, with this good Bishop is, his uncertainty whether the saints can have any knowledge of the petitions made to them, but this difficulty seems to be completely removed by the declaration of Scripture, that there is joy in heaven at the conversion of a sinner St. Augustine (Lib. de Cura pro Mort. c. 26,) moves the same difficulty, confessing it above the reach of his reason, to understand how the saints relieve those that call upon them. Yet he, with all the holy fathers and doctors of the church, maintains that the saints do certainly assist us, and intercede for such as call upon them.

Divine mysteries, as I have already observed, always offer difficulties to the human understanding. The present difficulty, however, is not altogether insuperable to human reason; on the contrary, dear sir, the Catholic belief on the present subject must, upon examination, meet the approbation of reason.

Would it not be unreasonable, even impious, to assert, that the saints and angels assisted with the light of grace and glory, do not know as much as the infernal spirits, who are deprived of both. Now, sir, it is certain that evil spirits have knowledge of us, and in a great measure know not only our actions, but even our thoughts.

The devil cometh, says Christ, and taketh the word out of their heart, lest believing they should be saved. Luke viii. 12. When an unclean spirit is gone out of a man, he walketh through dry places, seeking rest, and findeth none. Then he saith, I will return into my house from whence I came out. And coming he findeth it empty, swept, and garnished. Then he goeth, and taketh with him seven other spirits more wicked than himself, and they enter in and dwell there: and the last state of that man is made worse than the first, Matt. xii. 43, 44, 45. Moreover, since the evil spirit is said by St. John, to be 'the accuser of the servants of God,' Apoc. xii. 10, and by St. Peter, 'to be like a roaring lion going about, seeking whom he may devour,' 1 Pet. v. 8.

Is it unreasonable to believe, that blessed spirits have at least as much power in protecting man, as infernal spirits in destroying man? Is it unreasonable to believe, that the blessed spirits who surround the throne of God, have at least as much zeal for the salvation of man, as infernal spirits for his damnation? Finally, is it unreasonable to suppose, that the blessed in heaven are as able and willing to plead in our behalf, as evil spirits are to accuse us?

The secrets of hearts have been in many instances known to mortals. Thus, Eliseus, in his house, knew the king's intention to take his head, 4 Kings vi. 32. thus, the same Eliseus knew what passed between his servant Giezi and Naman, when himself was absent, 4 Kings v. 26.

St. Peter knew the sacrilegious fraud acted privately between Ananias and Saphira, Acts v. What was possible for feeble mortals, by the light of grace, should that be impossible for the blessed saints, who have both the light of grace and glory? Of whom St. Paul says, 'they see and know God face to face, even as they themselves are known,' 1 Cor. xiii. 12. Much more might be said on the subject; enough has been said to convince the candid reader that Catholics are not guilty of superstition in honouring those whom God himself chooses to honour, and in expecting much from the intercession and protection of those blessed angels and saints, who surround the throne of God, and whose thoughts, desires, affections, charity, zeal, &c. are in perfect unison with God's holy will and infinite charity.

It can be no superstition then, to believe, that the saints desire our salvation, because God desires it. It can be no superstition to believe, that the saints know our thoughts and desires, (which even the devils know,) the Scripture declaring that the repentance of the sinner on earth, causes joy among the blessed in heaven, Luc. xv. 10.

It can be no superstition to expect much from the protection of those, who, by the spirit of God are declared to be appointed ministering spirits for our salvation, Heb. i. 14. And who are again declared to have power, and to be rulers of nations,

Apoc. ii. 26. It can be no superstition to apply to the intercession of those, who in Holy Writ are declared intercessors in our behalf, Zach. i. and ii. Mac. xv. It can be no superstition to believe, that the intercession of the saints in heaven will be of more avail towards deciding the fate of men and nations, than the intercession of ten mortals would have been in deciding the fate of a city, Gen. xviii. 32. Or the intercession of one man (Job) in deciding the fate of his three friends.

Permit me, dear sir, to ask one question. Are you very certain, that the Lord, whose decrees are inscrutable, has not perhaps made your salvation dependent on the intercession of some certain saint or saints? Are you altogether certain, that your own prayers will prove sufficient to obtain now, and in your last hour, a full application of the merits of your dying Saviour? The Lord, it is true, is merciful beyond expression, but he calls himself a jealous God; are you certain, that the Lord is not offended, that his wrath is not kindled to the highest degree, at seeing those neglected and despised upon earth, whom he so much exalts and honours in heaven.

Are you certain, that those will ever be associated in the enjoyment of eternal glory, to the blessed saints in heaven, that had no communication with them on earth?

11*

The Apostles' creed, *I believe in God, &c.* makes mention of the *communion of saints,* which is the ninth article of this creed. Pray; which church is it that really, and not in words alone, holds and believes this communion of saints in every sense of the word?

Forgive me, dear sir, if my zeal for the salvation of my Protestant fellow-mortals causes me sometimes to overstep the bounds of my subject, and of my original plan, which was to exculpate Roman Catholics from the guilt of superstition. Before concluding, I must here observe with respect to this false and odious charge, that it was first made to serve the interested views of those who judged it expedient to excite clamour and prejudice against the Catholic religion. They well knew the falsehood of what they asserted, but wanting sufficient virtue to prefer truth to temporal advantages, they hesitated not to employ the vilest slanders to attain their end. The same are still propagated by many, either from the same base motive, or because they suppose this the surest and readiest means of bringing themselves into notice, or of acquiring influence in their respective societies, by thus gratifying the prejudices of their hearers. The conduct of the latter is scarcely less culpable than that of the former. It is a very weak excuse for those who now calumniate our religion, to say that they, finding those charges already made by others, take them for granted, without inquiring whether they are true or false. Such a mode of proceeding would be extremely unjust towards even an individual, and it is much more so, towards the far largest body of christians in existence. Our adversaries are so much the less excusable in imputing to us doctrines which we detest, as they might easily ascertain what we really hold, especially since so many approved works, containing the principles of our belief and practice, are before the public, and may be easily had. Some of them have so far misrepresented our invocation of the saints, as to charge us with substituting the worship of demons for that of God. The falsehood of this charge of idolatry, is evident from the simple statement of our doctrine on this point :— we believe that it is good and profitable to invoke the prayers of the saints, to whom God can, by innumerable ways, reveal those addressed to them ; and therefore, it is unimportant to know what may be the particular means employed by him for this end. By praying to them, we attribute no divine perfection to creatures, as the idolaters did, since we acknowledge even in the greatest saints, no degree of excellence, but what comes from God ; no virtue, but what is the gift of his grace ; no knowlege of human affairs, but what he is pleased to communicate to them ; in fine, no power of assisting us, except by their prayers. Moreover, that the saints are not raised above the rank of creatures, by ascribing to them the knowledge imparted, however, by God, not only of the things passing in this life, but even of our thoughts, is evident from the examples of the Prophets, who knew not only things present, but what is yet more wonderful, future things, the knowledge of which God seems to have particularly reserved to himself. Hence, several eminent Protestant writers, who have viewed, in its proper light, the doctrine of Catholics on this point, have totally given up the groundless charge of idolatry and superstition : for example, Bishop Montague, quoted above ; and Thorndike, prebendary of Westminster, warns his brethren 'not to lead people by the nose, to believe they can prove Papists to be idolaters, when they cannot,' Just Weights, p. 10.

I shall now in a few words explain the doctrine of the holy Catholic Church respecting images, pictures and relics.

ARTICLE VIII.

IMAGES, PICTURES AND RELICS.

Much indeed needs not be said on that subject to those who are candid, and provided with the least share of common sense; to those, who with seeing eyes will not see, and with hearing ears will not ear, too much has been said already.

The General Council of Trent declares, that 'the sacred bodies of the holy martyrs and of other saints, who were living members of Christ, and the temples of the Holy Ghost, which bodies will by him be raised to eternal life and glorified, ought to be venerated by the faithful on earth,' Conc. Trid. Ses. 25. 'Also, that the images of Christ, of the Blessed Virgin, and of other saints, are to be retained, especially in churches, and that *due honour* and veneration is to be given to them, not that any divinity or any power is believed to reside in them.' The Catechism of the Council of Trent adds, *istud maxime cavendum, ne quod Deo proprium est cuiquam præterae triburant*, T. 2, p. 603; particular care must be taken, that to none be given what belongs to God alone.

Here is nothing but what every christian must approve as conformable to the Word of God, and to reason.

St. John the Baptist venerated the very latchets of our Saviour's shoes. Mark i. 7.

The Israelites venerated the brazen serpent, a type or figure of Christ, Numb. xxi. 9.

By the command of God, two images of cherubim were made and placed on the ark, Exod. xxv 18. The primitive christians venerated the very shadows and garments of St. Peter and St. Paul, and received particular blessings thereby, Acts v. 15 and xix. 12.

Roman Catholics venerate the images of Christ, of the Blessed Virgin and of the saints, on account of their prototypes. None of them are so stupid as to believe that any divinity, any power or virtue resides in any of those images.

How many, both Protestants and Catholics, keep the picture of Gen. Washington, and exhibit the same in the most conspicuous place of their houses, certainly with a view of showing honour to the memory of the deceased general. Nobody, in his senses, ever thought of condemning that practice as superstitious.

How many Protestants hang upon the walls of their houses the pictures of their deceased parents and friends? How many a Protestant child will honour the picture of a deceased parent with a costly frame: look at that picture with sentiments of respect and veneration, perhaps bedew it with tears of sorrow and gratitude, nay, with the most sincere affection press it to its lips? Sir, will you accuse that child of superstition?

Let prejudice subside, and now substitute a Catholic in the room of the Protestant, and the picture of Christ crucified, in the place of the picture of the deceased parent; pray, dear sir, will you not permit that Catholic to exhibit his crucifix in the most conspicuous part of his house? Will you not permit him to look at his crucifix with respect and veneration? Will you not permit him to bedew his crucifix with tears of sorrow and gratitude? Nay, with the most sincere love and affection to press that crucifix to his lips? And suppose that Catholic should allow an honourable place to the picture of the most Blessed Virgin mother of our Saviour, and likewise to the pictures of the holy Apostles, and of the other servants of Christ, would you condemn him? Would you accuse him of superstition? I cannot think so.

I have spent many happy moments before the celebrated picture of Guido Reni, in the gallery of Dusseldorf in Germany, which represents the assumption of the Blessed Virgin, and I must confess that I was struck with awe. I found myself in a deep contemplation, my soul, as it were, withdrawn from its earthly habitation, and elevated towards the mansions of eternal bliss. The heavenly looks of the Virgin, as expressed in the picture, pointed out to me the proper object of my affections. With the deepest sentiments of my unworthiness, I had the most exalted ideas of the dignity of man, and it was with regret I left the spot, when called away to my lodgings.

Religious pictures in general, are well calculated both to enlighten and edify. To enlighten by exhibiting the most remarkable and prominent facts belonging to the history of religion; to edify by kindling up the fire of devotion.

What place then could be found more proper for religious pictures than the church, the house of God, the sanctuary, where the tremendous sacrifice is offered, and where the sacraments, the divine mysteries, are administered. That place, above all others, is the place of devotion, and it is there, that by hearing the word of God, by offering up our prayers, by meditating on divers religious subjects represented by our pictures, meditating on the religious and moral virtues of the saints, whose images are before us, meditating especially on the great sufferings of Christ, as represented by our crucifixes, on his immense love for sinners, &c. it is there, I say, and by such means, that our piety is both enlightened and inflamed.

Superstition!!! Amiable superstition indeed, which is productive of so much good. And does not zeal for the cause of religion suggest a sincere desire, that the crucifix and other religious pictures would be substituted in the place of many of those pictures that often adorn the walls of our people of fashion, to the detriment of both religion and morals? Would not that zeal which attacks our religious pictures, and exhibits them most shamefully as the objects of our superstitious worship, be more meritoriously employed in condemning those indecent, immodest and truly scandalous pictures, which by defiling the imagination, and tarnishing the purity of the heart, are so calculated to extinguish devotion, or the love of God altogether, and therefore to produce an effect the very reverse of that produced by religious pictures: and if the commandment of God, 'thou shalt not make to thyself any graven image,' &c. ever was intended to be understood in the literal sense, was it not principally with regard to such images or pictures, as have a tendency, by defiling the imagination, and corrupting the heart, to withdraw from the great Creator that affection, honour and worship which are due to him alone, and to place them on the most unworthy of God's creatures. This, in my opinion, is the most dangerous kind of idolatry, the most universally practised, both by bad Catholics and bad Protestants. It is thus the idolatry of the Pagans chiefly originated; never would altars have been erected to Bacchus or to Venus, had not corrupted man bestowed his heart and affections on the infamous objects of his passions.

Ah sir! permit me to say it, this is not one of the least of Satan's infernal stratagems, in order to drag millions of souls into the gulf of perdition to raise the hue and cry against Popish pictures, Popish idolatry, to sound the trumpet of alarm from the rising to the setting of the sun, and to attack the pious practice of keeping crucifixes and religious pictures, with sharp and poisonous shafts of low ribaldry and sarcasm. I say this is not one of the least of Satan's infernal stratagems, in order to divert the attention of corrupted man from the far more dangerous idolatry in which his own heart is engaged, having bestowed all his attention, his affection, his devotion on the unworthy objects of his criminal passions, and feeling for his God nothing but the most perfect indifference.

That gentlemen who call themselves ministers of Christ, who pretend to no inconsiderable share of learning, and who are, or might be well acquainted with the doctrine and practice of the Catholic Church, in regard to crucifixes and pictures, should join in this work of destruction, should wilfully misrepresent this pious and edifying doctrine and practice, and that they should, with unabated zeal, attack this pretended Popish idolatry, a mere phantom, instead of directing their united efforts against that real idolatry, which is driving millions of souls into the gulf of perdition, is truly astonishing, and affords an additional proof of what I have already advanced, that sinful man, if he should become so presumptuous as to attempt reforming the most holy, the most perfect of all the works of God, the church, will, in just punishment for his sacrilegious presumption, be deprived of the heavenly light of God's grace; with seeing eyes he will not see, he will call right wrong, and wrong right, and 'blaspheming what he does not know, he will perish in his own corruption,' 2 Pet. ii. 12.

With regard to relics or remains of saints, we honour them in the same way as we do religious images, according to the practice of antiquity. If this practice scandalizes you, sir, why do you permit your Protestant hearers to show honour and respect to the remains or relics of their deceased friends? Are not the remains or relics of your deceased Protestants honoured with decent burials, accompanied with many ceremonies? Are not their tombs decorated with costly monuments? Are not the remains or relics of many Protestants embalmed at very great expense, and sometimes even with great labour and cost, conveyed many thousand miles to the country of their nativity, to be deposited with great pomp and ceremony in the burying ground of the family? Is not this paying respect and honour to remains and relics; such respect and honour are frequently shown by both Catholics and Protestants, without incurring the guilt of superstition, though shewn to the remains or relics of men often notorious for their impiety!!! To the remains or relics of men. who, though entitled by their services, to the gratitude of their country, yet in all their life-time, never seemed to remember their Saviour, only to blaspheme his holy name, and who have left us, to say the very best, in the most cruel uncertainty, with regard to their future and everlasting destiny, having nothing to found our hopes on, but the late, commonly too late, repentance of the agonizing sinner!!!

Now, sir, if such honour and respect may be shown to the relics of men, whose souls have received that sentence which their deeds deserved, and are actually a prey to God's eternal vengeance, why shall it be a sin, why superstition, to shew honour and respect to the relics of men, who, having been the best among the good, the holiest among the holy, are now enjoying in the bosom of God, the fruits of their penance and charity, sanctified by the merits of their Saviour? Why shall it be superstition to venerate and honour the relics or remains of the Apostles, whose sacred bodies underwent such great fatigues, labours and sufferings, in order to administer salvation to the different nations of the globe? Why superstition to respect and venerate the sacred remains of so many thousands of martyrs, whose souls and bodies were altogether employed in promoting the glory of God, and the salvation of their fellow-mortals, who died under the most excruciating torments, victims of their faith and charity?

How much Almighty God is pleased with the honour rendered to the relics of his deceased servants and saints, he has repeatedly proved by making these very relics instruments of miracles.

The very touch of Eliseu's bones raised a dead man to life, 4 Kings xiii. 21.

The napkins and handkerchiefs, that had but touched the body of St. Paul, cast out devils and cured diseases, Acts xix. 12.

Nay, the very shadow of St. Peter, cured diseases in such as honoured it, Acts v. 15.

St. Augustin, a holy father, respected by both Protestants and Catholics, certifies, that at the relics of St. Stephen, there were so many miracles wrought, that if all should be recorded, they would fill many volumes, Book 22, of the City of God.

When we consider, that the body of a christian is, in a great measure, made partaker of those blessings, which by the holy sacraments of the church, are conveyed to his soul, and that at the general resurrection, it will likewise partake of that divine glory, with which the mercy of God will reward his faithful servants, we must readily confess, that a great deal of honour, respect and veneration, is due to the remains or relics of a saint.

The water of regeneration administered in baptism, sanctifies the body as well as the soul, and renders it susceptible through the merits of Christ of eternal glory.

In the holy sacrament of confirmation, it is sanctified again by the presence of the Holy Ghost, and the anointing with the holy chrism.

By means of that body we eat the flesh of Christ, who thus communicates himself to the soul.

Thus, a body, nothing but clay, and by the sin of Adam, nothing but corruption, becomes through the merits of the Redeemer, a sanctified body, the temple of the Holy Ghost, 1 Cor. vi. 19. The mansion of Christ, destined to become at the general resurrection a spiritual body, a glorified body, resplendent with light and glory for ever, 1 Cor. xv. 43, 44.

Is it superstition, dear sir, to show great respect and veneration to those remains or relics, which God himself is pleased to honour so highly? But you have been told, or you have read somewhere, that Catholics worship relics! Of this I do not doubt, for I have been told so repeatedly, and have read it in several Protestant books; yet, although I lived fifteen years in a Catholic country, and have been acquainted with numbers of Catholics, both of the clergy and laity from almost every Catholic country in Europe, I never knew one so stupid as to worship relics. The most ignorant can easily distinguish the supreme worship due to God alone, from the respect to be shown to the relics of the saints, his servants. If this relative respect may, as we have shown, be lawfully paid to the memorials of all distinguished persons, why may it not be equally so to those of the saints? Veneration has been maintained for them in all ages of the church, for we know that the primitive christians carried away the relics of St. Ignatius, St. Polycarp, and other martyrs, immediately after their execution, and carefully preserved them as more valuable than gold and precious stones. It appears from St Gregory of Nyssa, who lived in the fourth age, that the relics of the saints were deposited in the churches. Hence, according to the custom of venerable antiquity, those precious relics are kept in costly shrines under and about the altars, and highly venerated, as having been even in their corruptible state, the temple of the Holy Ghost, 1 Cor. vi. 19, and as being intended for eternal glory, when re-united to the soul.

I shall now dismiss the subject, trusting that I have said more than enough to convince you and your candid hearers, that we are by no means guilty of superstition, in respecting and honouring the images and relics of saints. The principal article of importance left for me to explain, is what we believe of the Pope.

ARTICLE IX.

THE POPE.

We believe that Jesus Christ, who would have his church to be one, and solidly built upon unity, hath instituted the primacy of St. Peter, to support and to cement it.

To St. Peter alone, our blessed Saviour said, 'thou art Peter (a rock) and upon this rock I will build my church,' &c. Matt. xvi. 18.

To Peter alone, our blessed Saviour said, 'I will give to thee the keys of the kingdom of heaven,' &c. ver. 19.

To Peter alone, our blessed Saviour said, 'I have prayed for thee that thy faith fail not; and thou being once converted, confirm thy brethren,' Luc. xxii. 32.

To Peter alone, our blessed Saviour proposed three times the following question, 'Simon, son of Jonas, lovest thou me?' John xxi. 15, 16, 17, and upon Peter's answer in the affirmative, he tells him twice, 'feed my lambs,' and the third time, 'feed my sheep.' Finally,

Although Jesus Christ tells all his Apostles collectively, 'whatsoever you shall bind on earth, shall be bound also in heaven, and whatsoever you shall loose upon earth, shall be loosed also in heaven,' Matt. xviii. 18. Yet Peter is the only one, who receives the power separately and individually, 'I will give to thee the keys of the kingdom of heaven, and whatsoever thou shalt bind upon earth,' &c. Matt. xvi. 19.

The name of Peter is generally mentioned before the names of the other Apostles, although it appears, that others were called to the apostleship before him; and we find upon all important occasions, Peter taking the lead among the Apostles. In the choice of an Apostle to supply the vacancy occasioned by the prevarication of Judas, Acts i. 15; in the first sermon preached in Jerusalem, after the coming of the Holy Ghost, Acts ii. 14; in the first miraculous cure, Acts iii. 4—6; in the defence before the high priests, Acts iv.; in the judgment against Ananias and Saphira, Acts v.; in the calling of the Gentiles to the church of Christ, Acts x.; likewise in the first council held at Jerusalem, Acts xv. 7.

This primacy of jurisdiction, which was given to St. Peter, we acknowledge in the successors of St. Peter, the bishops of Rome, to this present day. Their names are all upon record, and any person versed in the history of the church, and the writings of the holy fathers, will candidly confess, that a primacy of jurisdiction has always been acknowledged in the bishops of Rome.

St. Irenæus, in the second age, says, 'that all churches, round about, ought to resort to the Roman Church, by reason of its more powerful principality,' L. iii. c. 3.

In the third age, St. Cyprian says, 'we hold Peter the head and root of the church,' and he calls the church of Rome, 'St. Peter's chair,' Epist. 55.

In the fourth age, St. Basil calls St. Peter, 'that blessed one, who was preferred before the rest of the Apostles,' Serm. de Judicio Dei.

In the same age, St. Epiphanius says, 'he chose Peter to be the chief of his disciples,' Heres. 51.

In the same age, again, St. Cyril of Jerusalem, says, 'Peter the prince, and most excellent of all the Apostles,' Catechis. 2.

In the same age, St. Chrysostom says, 'the pastor and head of the church was once a poor fisherman,' Homil. 55 in Matt.

In the same age, Eusebius Emissenus calls St. Peter 'not only pastor, but the pastor of pastors,' Serm. de Nativ. S. Jo.

Again, St. Ambrose says, 'Andrew first followed our Saviour, yet Andrew received not the primacy, but Peter,' in 2 Cor. xii.

In the fifth age, St. Augustin calls 'Peter the head of the Apostles, the gate-keeper of heaven, and the foundation of the church,' (*to wit*, under Christ,) Epist. 86.

The first General Council of Nice, A. D. 325, defined, that 'he who holds the See of Rome, is the head and chief of all the patriarchs —— as being the vicar of Christ our Lord over all people, and the universal church of Christ, and whosoever shall contradict this, is excommunicated.'

The same is declared by the General Council of Chalcedon, Sess. 15, Can. 58, A. D. 451. And in all subsequent general councils down to the last, the General Council of Trent, A. D. 1545, the bishop of Rome, with the unanimous consent of all the bishops always presided.

Several learned Protestant divines own this primacy of the church of Rome, and acknowledge its usefulness.

Hugo Grotius, a celebrated Protestant divine, who was very industrious in examining into the root of all Protestant divisions, and very zealous in composing them, positively declares in his last work, written shortly before his death, 'that there can be no hopes of uniting Protestants among themselves, except they are united together with those who are in communion with the See of Rome,' Close of last reply to Rivet.

Melancthon likewise confesses that 'the primacy is even necessary for preserving unity.'

'What is the reason (says the above quoted Grotius' reply to Rivet, ad Art. 7,) that those among Catholics, who differ in opinion, still remain in the same body, without breaking communion, and those among the Protestants who disagree, cannot do so, however they speak much of brotherly love? Whoever will consider this aright, will find how great is the effect of primacy.'

'As certain bishops (says Melancthon) preside over many churches, so the bishop of Rome is president over all bishops. And this canonical policy, no wise man, I think, does or ought to disallow, for the monarchy of the bishop of Rome is, in my judgment, profitable to this end, that consent of doctrine may be retained. Wherefore an agreement may easily be established in this article of the Pope's supremacy, if other articles could be agreed upon,' Cent. Epist. Theol. 74.

Mr. Thorndike, another celebrated Protestant divine, confesses that 'a pre-eminency of power and not of rank only, has been acknowledged originally in the church of Rome,' Epic. L. 3, cap. 20, p. 179.

I have in my possession a letter, written by Martin Luther to Pope Leo the tenth, dated A. D. 1518, and printed among the other works of Luther, in Jena, A. D. 1579, vol. i. p. 74. This document is of so much the more importance as it proves beyond the possibility of a doubt, that

Martin Luther, the father of the pretended Reformation, at the date of the letter, acknowledged the bishop of Rome as the head of the church, and his lawful superior, and that if he afterwards rejected the same authority, it was evidently the effect of passion, spite and malice, produced by the sentence of excommunication, which the Pope pronounced against him; in this we are confirmed by the indecent, scurrilous and malicious language made use of by Luther after his excommunication, whenever he speaks of the Pope.

I shall only quote two passages of Luther's letters to the Pope, the beginning and the conclusion.

Epistola Lutheri ad Leonem X. Rom. Pont. Beatissimo patri Leoni Decimo Pont. Max. F. Martinus Lutherus Augastinianus æternam salutem.

'*Auditum audivi de me passinum Beatissime Pater, quo intelligi, quosdam amicos fecisse nomen meum gravissime coram te et tuis fœtere, ut quia auctoritatem et potestatem clavium, et summi pontificis minuere molitus sim —— sed rem ipsam, Beatissime Pater, digneres audire ex me,*' &c.

In English:

Epistle of Luther to Leo X. Roman Pontiff

To the most holy father Leo the tenth, sovereign Pontiff, brother Martin Luther of the order of St. Augustine, wishes eternal welfare.

'I am informed, most holy father, that you have heard of me the very worst, and understand that certain friends have brought my name into very bad repute before you, &c., saying that I am trying to lessen the authority and power of the keys and of the sovereign Pontiff —— but deign, most holy father, to hear the whole business from me,' &c.

Luther concludes the letter with the following words:

'*Quare, Beatissime Pater, prostratum me pedibus tuæ beatitudinis offero cum omnibus, quæ sum et habeo. Vivifica, occide, voca, revoca, approba, reproba, ut placuerit; vocem tuam, vocem Christi in te præsidentis et loquentis agnoscam,*' &c. In English:

'Therefore, most holy father, prostrate at the feet of your holiness, I offer myself and all I have. Vivify, kill, call, recall, approve or reprove as you please, in your voice I acknowledge the voice of Christ, who presides and speaks to you,' &c.*

---

* Such was the language of Luther till his doctrine was condemned, when he shook off all authority, and set up the tribunal of his own private judgment. No sooner had he done so than his disciples, proceeding on the same principle, undertook to prove that his own doctrine was erroneous. Carlstadt, Zuinglius, Occolampadius, Muncer, and several others

I shall not be detained in defending the temporal power exercised by some Popes. That the Pope has any such power, was never an article of faith. It is true that this power has been assumed and exercised. Yet candour requires that we should view history as it is in itself, and not as it appears through the prism of misrepresentation. When ignorance and barbarity, which were the natural consequences of the dissolution of the Roman empire, and of the invasion of the

of his followers, wrote and preached against him and against each other with the utmost virulence. In vain did he claim a superiority over them; in vain did he denounce hell-fire against them; he had the mortification to see his assumed authority, as well as threats, totally disregarded by them. His followers continued to act in open defiance of him, till their mutual abuse became so scandalous as to fill the more moderate among them with grief and shame. Experience convinced them that for preserving unity of faith, and regularity of discipline, a fixed supreme authority is required. Capito, minister of Strasburg, writing to Farel, pastor of Geneva, thus complains to him, ' God has given me to understand the mischief we have done, by our precipitancy in breaking with the Pope,' &c. Dudith, another Reformer, writing to Beza, says, ' in what single point are those churches which have declared war against the Pope, agreed amongst themselves ?'

barbarians, had spread all over Europe, national and civil wars were the order of the day. Nations were arrayed against nations, kings and emperors against each other; myriads of petty chieftains, each one with his retinue, were laying waste the whole face of Europe. No safety was to be found; but destruction, violence, murder and bloodshed were to be met with every where. Among the laity there were none who knew how, or were willing or able to administer justice. In that general desolation, it was but natural that both the people and their chiefs should turn their attention towards the See of Peter, on which sat men to whom their eminent virtue and science gave a moral influence which placed them above all their contemporaries. All were anxious to take refuge under their protection. It was not the Popes who sought for power, but it was power which forced itself, as it were, upon the Popes. The people were like children calling on their common father to preserve them from destruction. Had the Pope turned a deaf ear to their call, he would have been accused of egotism and indifference; he protected them, and he is accused of ambition, of thirst of power, &c. as well might a young man who has become of age, accuse his guardian of ambition, because during his infancy, he watched over his interests.

It is a remarkable fact, that whenever the Pope

has exercised that temporal power which is the object of so much and so bitter censure, he has exercised it for the interest of the people against their oppressors, by deciding that they were no longer, in conscience, bound to obey those princes who instead of acting the part of fathers towards their subjects, had become their insufferable tyrants. It is also remarkable, that in those memorable occasions, when the Pope is said to have deprived princes of their dominions, it was never for his own benefit, and they never acquired an inch of ground for themselves.

In short, the exercise of that power was grounded on the general jurisprudence of those times, and princes themselves contributed and gave sanction to it, by frequently applying to the holy See for the settlement of their temporal concerns. Thus, the accusation of ambition, pride, &c. against the Popes, disappears, when the facts are accurately investigated, and truly stated.

What is called the patrimony of St. Peter, is an estate which the Pope owes to the munificence of his powerful friends, and which he has possessed for upwards of a thousand years; and when he has taken up arms, it has been either to protect it against aggressors, or to rescue it from the hands of those who had invaded it unjustly.

I shall never try to defend the conduct of all our Popes. Peter denied his master; is it a won der then if among so many of his successors, some should be found guilty of prevarications? Some, no doubt, were far from being edifying in their conduct. Christ foresaw it; what he says of the Pharisees and Jewish doctors may be said of them. The Pharisees and Scribes have sitten upon the chair of Moses. All therefore whatsoever they shall say unto you, observe and do; but according to their works do ye not, Matt. xviii. 2, 3.

Although in their capacity as men, some Popes have exhibited proofs of their weakness and corruption, yet as heads of the church, they have all during these eighteen hundred years taught one and the same Catholic doctrine.

If the abuse of power were conclusive against the title of him who exercises it, there would be no longer any authority upon earth. On the contrary, I may safely advance, that the real or supposed abuse of power by some Popes, not only proves nothing against the solidity of their title, but is an argument in favour of its existence.

If we take a retrospective view of the history of the world, we shall find that abuses of power have almost always been attended with the destruction of the power in which they originated. Thus the abuse of regal power turned Rome into a republic; the abuse of republican power, turned republican Rome into imperial Rome. Thus the abuse of imperial power turned Switzerland and other countries of Europe into republics, by abolishing the authority abused. Thus the abuse of English power turned the United States into a republic, by abolishing in these States the power of England.

What is the reason then that the abuses of papal power, supposing them to be as great and numerous as you represent them to be, have not been attended with the same consequences, the destruction of the papal power itself? Why does that power, after a lapse of eighteen hundred years, still continue to be acknowledged by three-fourths of christendom.

Christ gives the answer to this interesting query; 'Thou art Peter, and upon this rock I will build my church, and the gates of hell shall not prevail against it,' Matt. 16—18.

Attacked with the most relentless fury for ages, by the combined efforts of hell and earth, by fierce enemies in and out of the Catholic Church apparently on the brink of destruction, its down fall has often been prophesied.

Many of the sovereign Pontiffs fell victims to those persecutions. The majestic rock of St. Peter remained, Peter was put to death. Pius the VII. was banished and kept in close confinement. During the period of about eighteen hundred years, from Peter to Pius the VII. the chair of St

Peter has still been occupied, and we have upon the records of the Catholic Church, the names of more than two hundred and fifty sovereign Pontiffs, who followed one another in regular succession, on the chair of St. Peter; a great number of whom died martyrs for their faith, very few of whom can be said to have been scandalous.

Mr. Hume, who certainly will not be suspected of partiality for the Catholic religion, owns that although 'the Popes sometimes misused the authority they had, they most commonly made a laudable and humane use of it, by promoting peace among christian princes, by uniting them against the hordes of barbarians who were extending every day their bloody conquests, by repressing simony, violence and every kind of excess, which overbearing, cruel masters committed against their weak, oppressed subjects; it served to make, of the whole christian world, one great family, whose differences were adjusted by one common father, the Pontiff of the God of concord and justice. A grand and affecting idea that, of the most extensive and the noblest administration that could be thought of.'

From what I have stated, you will plainly see, dear sir, that all that can be alleged of the criminal conduct or abuse of power of some Popes, makes nothing against the Catholic Church. It only proves that Popes are subject to human frailties in common with the rest of mankind; that with the Roman orator, they have a right to say, '*homo sum, humani nihil a me alienum puto;*' and that no power or authority, how great soever; no character, how sacred soever; affords sufficient security against the corruption of human nature, and the influence of the passions.

Far from affording an argument against the Catholic Church, I rather think that the corruption of Popes, and of the clergy, admitting it to exist even beyond the limits our adversaries would fain wish to suppose, affords a powerful argument in favour of the Catholic Church.

Any person possessing the least knowledge of the nature of man, and versed in the history of religion, will own that religious opinions have but too often originated in the passions and the corrupted heart of man, their dictates being too often mistaken for those of cool and impartial reason: neither will it be denied that the great variety of religious systems (which may be counted by hundreds) contradicting and condemning one another, owe their origin to the variety of human passions and interests. Before the coming of Christ, the objects of religious worship were more spiritual, or more carnal, according to the impulse given to the hearts of men, by their respective passions, either towards spiritual or carnal objects. The world embracing christianity, has introduced into the church its corruption and its passions. Although men ruled by the same passions, are, by the overwhelming force of evidence, prevented from mistaking the main object of their worship, which is Jesus Christ, yet being under the influence of these various passions and interests, they pretend to find out various ways of going to Jesus, ways more easy, more smooth, in short more congenial to each one's passions and inclinations; ways more spiritual or more carnal, ways all differing from the old narrow road which alone was pointed out by Jesus Christ as leading to him. Now, sir, starting from this undeniable position, and admitting Popes, clergy, and if you choose, lay-people of the Catholic Church by millions, to have been very much corrupted, the Popes and clergy to have been ruled by pride, ambition, covetousness, and all the passions that corrupted hearts are subject to; to have set up and enforced the most extravagant claims, to have with Satan equalled themselves to the Most High; if notwithstanding this sink of corruption, if notwithstanding the wonderful irritation and opposition which such tyrannical claims and acts must have produced, if notwithstanding this dreadful conflict of passions and clashing of interest, the Catholic Church has still continued to this day during a period of eighteen centuries, to preserve its perfect unity, has still continued to acknowledge the same power, and the same head, though guilty of such enormous abuses, must we not confess, that here is the hand of the Most High?

Travel over all the Catholic countries of Europe, why has the demon of discord, who has so many times overturned their governments by the most dreadful revolutions; why have the furious tempests raised by human passions, that have divided, destroyed, leveled with the ground so many human institutions, that seemed to bid defiance to time; why have they not been able to divide, to destroy Catholic unity, to hurl the Pope from the See of St. Peter; to emancipate Catholics from the tyrannical yoke (as it is called) of the Roman Pontiffs?

The answer is plain.

The Catholic Church, the See of St. Peter, Catholic unity, are all the work of God, which man cannot destroy.

Popes, Bishops and Priests, as individuals, are subject to all the passions, and form of themselves nothing but a dead body, which, like any other human body, would soon become a prey to corruption and dissolution, were it not, according to the promise of Jesus Christ, animated, vivified and preserved forever in perfect unity by the holy spirit of truth. The Holy Ghost being the soul of that body, keeps it alive, keeps it, head and members, in unity and harmony. Being itself the foundation of truth and holiness, it dispels the mists of falsehood and corruption, which the malice of Satan and the passions of individuals, whether clergy or lay-people, often cause to arise in order to obscure the bright and pure rays of Divine revelation. Thus the abuses in the church, whether in the members or the head, are reformed by the church, and the words of Christ accomplished, 'the gates of hell shall not prevail against it,' &c.

I shall take but little time to refute the false and ridiculous charge of those who accuse our Popes of granting indulgences to commit sin, requiring a certain sum of money, greater or smaller, according to the kind of sin for which the indulgence is granted.

That such a charge is frequently published in Protestant books, and from Protestant pulpits, you will not deny. Now, all Catholic books, sanctioned by the church, no matter where or when published, tell you plainly, that an indulgence is nothing but a remission or relaxation of certain temporal punishments, remaining due to sin, after the guilt and eternal punishment are remitted, as in the case of David, to whom Nathan said, 'the Lord hath taken away thy sin; nevertheless —— the child that is born to thee shall surely die,' 2 Kings xii. 13, 14.

Such indulgences are granted upon the sinner's

sincere repentance, and satisfaction for his past sins; the Apostles and their successors having received from Christ full authority to forgive the sins of those who are judged worthy of forgiveness. There is no doubt, but owing to the perverseness of many individuals among the clergy, the most shocking abuses have taken place sometimes in the dispensation of indulgences; however, as these abuses were not sanctioned, but reprobated by the church, as you can see if you read chap. ix. of the 21st Sess. and *Decretum de Indulgentiis* of the 25th Sess. of the Council of Trent, they of course make nothing against the holiness, purity and infallibility of the church of Christ, and only prove, that all human flesh is subject to infirmities.

I believe, dear sir, that I have fulfilled my promise, and proved to every body's satisfaction, that Roman Catholics are not guilty of superstition in submitting to the spiritual jurisdiction of St. Peter and of his successors, the sovereign Pontiffs or Bishops of Rome.

Permit me to add a few words more on another important subject, on which our doctrine is grossly misrepresented, I mean the doctrine of the Catholic Church on toleration.

ARTICLE X.

TOLERATION.

We are represented as the most intolerant set of men upon earth. The most cruel, the most uncharitable intolerance is laid to our charge;*

---

* A favourite topic with most Protestant writers, is, to charge the Catholic Church with a spirit of persecution. They constantly describe her as intolerant, and as claiming the right of punishing those who differ from her, with fire and sword. This is a malicious accusation, intended to excite hatred against her. The Catholic Church neither does, nor ever did claim any such right. Persecuting laws, it is true, have been made and acted upon by several Catholic princes, who, for the most part, judged such necessary to preserve the ancient order of things, and prevent the anarchy which attended reforming principles Is it fair then, to ascribe what has been done, chiefly from motives of state policy, to the persecuting spirit of the church? But has not persecution been practised by Protestants in every country in which they have acquired power; and this not only against Catholics, but even fellow Protestants? Witness the conduct of the first settlers in New England. It may here be asked, can our accusers show in the statutes of any Catholic country, any to be compared with the demoralizing and inhuman penal laws of England and Ireland? What Catholics have for centuries suffered from religious persecution in this latter country alone, may be safely said to counterbalance all that Protestants have suffered on the score of religion throughout the rest of the world. Such writers then as represent the Catholic religion as essentially intolerant, and the but this charge against us probably proceeds from a misunderstanding of our doctrine on that subject.

The question here is not about civil toleration. Catholics and Protestants are united in considering civil toleration an invaluable blessing, especially in a country like ours, where there were so many different denominations at the time its constitution was formed. We all agree in believing, that no authority, merely human, possesses any right of controlling the consciences of men.

The question then before us is concerning theological toleration, *viz.* whether Almighty God can approve of so many different religious systems, which we find established upon earth; whether all these different religious systems can be considered as so many different ways to heaven. If so, we ought to be in favour of universal toleration.

The Catholic Church teaches, that Jesus Christ established but one church for the salvation of man, and that out of that one church salvation is not to be had.

The written word is very plain on this subject: 'There shall be made one fold and one pastor,' John x. 16. 'I beseech you, that you all speak

---

Protestant as alone admitting toleration, shows any thing but candour. It would seem that they either have unaccountably forgotten the existence of the above laws, still in several instances acted upon, or imagined their readers so ignorant, as not to know that such existed.

one thing, and that there be no schisms among you, but that you be perfect in one sense and one judgment,' 1 Cor. i. 10.

Christ prayed that his disciples might be one, John xvii. 11.

'One Lord, one faith, one baptism,' Ephes. iv. 5. 'He that believeth not shall be condemned,' Mar. xvi. 16. 'Without faith it is impossible to please God,' Heb. xi. 6.

'I believe one holy Catholic and Apostolic Church,' says the Nicene Creed, which is admitted by both Catholics and Protestants.

'This is the Catholic faith,' (says the Creed of St. Athanasius, likewise admitted by Catholics and Protestants,) 'which if any one does not faithfully and firmly believe, he cannot be saved.'

Several creeds and professions of faith which I have carefully perused, very plainly and unequivocally assert, that out of the church, which is but one, salvation cannot be obtained: so says the church of England, so says the church of Scotland, &c. What, indeed, can be more reasonable? And what, on the other hand, more unreasonable, more absurd, than universal toleration? To be convinced of it, it is only necessary to examine what true religion is.

True religion is an institution of which God himself is the founder. It is an institution in which God makes known to man what he must believe, and what he must do in order to obtain salvation. It is a system, not the offspring of human reason, not the result of human philosophy, not the ingenious contrivance of human talents and learning; it originates in the fountain of eternal and infinite wisdom, and was by the supreme authority of God, established on earth, to control both the understanding and the will of man, dictating to his understanding what he must believe, and to his will what he must submit to do in order to obtain salvation. It will not be denied, that God has as much right to control our understanding, to require a submission of our understanding to the belief of whatever mysteries he chooses to reveal, as he has to control our will to submit to his commandments. It will be also acknowledged, that God alone can save man, that God alone can institute a religion, worthy of himself, and adequate to supply all the spiritual wants and necessities of man, a religion, in which all those heavenly blessings are administered, which transform the carnal into a spiritual man, and finally into a citizen of heaven. God alone can draw man out of the mire of original corruption, and he alone has a right to determine by what means this wonderful change from depravity to innocence is to take place. None can attach to the weak element of water the power of performing this astonishing change.

None but God can wash away the iniquities of man, can restore to him his sanctifying grace, and none, except him, has a right to determine the means by, and the conditions upon which, this blessing of reconciliation and forgiveness is to be granted

None but God can feed and nourish the soul of man, or arm that soul with power sufficient to overcome his spiritual enemies, and to persevere to the last breath in the performance of his duty, and in the service of his Creator.

In short, sir, whatever blessings we stand in need of none but God can convey them, or determine the precise manner in which we are to obtain them. To say that man, even the wisest man, may by the force of reasoning, contrive a religious system, calculated to answer the above purposes, is to equal him to God.

Religion, then, is that divine institution of God's own creation, in which is shown to man the way to glorify God, and to procure everlasting happiness to his own soul. In it are established by Jesus Christ, certain rites or ceremonies, as so many channels to convey to our souls those manifold blessings, which we stand in need of. Those rites are called sacraments, and must be precisely the very thing that Jesus Christ instituted. If they are only of the institution of man, they are no longer entitled to religious respect, as man has not the power to annex heavenly blessings to the performing of certain external acts. I shall explain this general position by a few examples.

Jesus Christ has annexed, to the pouring of water on a person, and the pronouncing of the words, 'I baptize thee in the name of the Father, and of the Son, and of the Holy Ghost,' the grace of cleansing that person from the guilt of original sin. So we are told by the church, the infallible interpreter of God's word.

Pray, sir, would it be in the power of man to substitute some other words and ceremonies, and to make them equally efficacious in conveying the same blessing? I believe not. Jesus Christ has annexed to the words, *absolvo te a peccatis tuis*, (I absolve thee from thy sins,) when pronounced by a lawful successor of the Apostles, the power of really remitting sins, provided the sinner is well disposed. So we are told again by the infallible interpreter of God's word. Pray, sir, would it be in the power of man to give the same efficacy to some other words of his own contrivance? I think not.

Jesus Christ has annexed to the imposition of hands by legally consecrated bishops, and to the pronouncing of certain words, the power of communicating the Holy Ghost, which rite we call the sacrament of confirmation. So we are told again by the church Is it in the power of man by some other ceremonies and words of his own contrivance, to impart the Spirit of God to his fellow-mortals? Certainly not.

It is obvious then, that none but the one system of religion, which Jesus Christ himself established, is entitled to any religious respect whatever. In that one alone are to be found the true Scripture, the true interpreter of Scripture, the true word of God, the true sacrifice, the true sacraments; only in that one system of religion are to be found the true ministry of Christ, the power of the keys, &c. Reform that system of religion in one only point and you deform it, you change the work of God into the work of man. Denominate this doctrine uncharitable, cruel, barbarous, or whatever you please, it is beyond all doubt the doctrine of truth and common sense, and of course, the only one which genuine charity will make use of, because it is the duty of charity, to lead along the thorny paths of truth, and not along the enchanting and flowery roads of falsehood and deception. I here appeal not to your learning, not to your genius and talents, but only to your common sense, which enables you to know, that black is not white; and I ask you, whether it be uncharitable to teach that contradictory systems of religion cannot all proceed from the holy spirit of truth; whether it be uncharitable to say, that of a hundred religious systems contradicting one another in some point or other, only one can possibly be true, only one can proceed from the spirit of truth? When we hear one minister preaching up the necessity of baptism for salvation, and another promising salvation without baptism, is it uncharitable to say, that one of them is the minister of error, and not of Christ? When we hear one minister declare infants not admissible to baptism, and another, on the contrary, insisting on the necessity of baptizing infants, is it uncharitable to say, that one must be a teacher of error?

Is it uncharitable to say, that if Calvin is right, Luther must be wrong; if Arminius teacheth the truth, Gomar must be a teacher of falsehood; if Socinus is the teacher of pure and undefiled truth, Luther, Calvin, Arminius, Melancthon, Fox, Zuinglius, &c. &c. must all be ministers of error.

Or will it be more charitable, (adding blasphemy to deception,) to say, as the independent minister appears to do, page 58, that all these different teachers, although contradicting one another in most essential points, are all ministers of the God of truth? He makes mention of no less than seventy odd names of persons who were raised, he says, by the Almighty, from the seventh to the sixteenth century, to oppose the errors of the church of Rome, many of whom differed more from one another in matters of faith, than they did from the Catholic Church. It appears then that he, with many more of his colleagues, admits but one criterion of the true faith, *viz.* that of *protesting* against the holy Catholic Church. Thus when Luther pleads the necessity of baptism, and the real presence of Christ in the eucharist, he will say, *the man is right.* When Fox rejects baptism, eucharist, and all other sacraments, he, with the political Tinker, will say again, *the man is right.* When Calvin, differing from both, sees nothing in the eucharist but signs or symbols of the flesh and blood of Christ, again he will say, *the man is right.*

When Wickliff rises up against almost all divine and human institutions, and tries to establish his abominable system of liberty and independence, which caused so much blood to flow, here again, '*the man is right.*'

The independent minister, and I believe, all our modern ministers, those I mean, who would appear liberal, charitable, and I suppose, fashionable, will tell you, that all those men, and many more, were true ministers of God. They will tell you, forsooth, that they evinced their divine mission by opposing, by *protesting* against the church of Rome.

Thus is common sense sacrificed at the shrine of spite and malice, and a most impious, blasphemous system, a compound of the most palpable contradictions, obtruded on the ignorant and the prejudiced, as the pure religion of Jesus, under the name of *Protestant religion.*

Here are toleration and liberality extending to all sorts of creeds, but excluding the greatest number of the christian people.

You will hardly call such a toleration and liberality charitable, as on the one hand it makes too many exceptions, and on the other hand, as I have proved, it is not founded upon truth, and cannot meet the approbation of common sense; it is a deceptive kind of charity, it calls out peace, peace, and there is no peace; it lulls the unhappy sinner into false security, and under the pompous names of Reformation, Protestantism, &c. leads him far away from the only true church of Jesus Christ.

Catholic intolerance is both rational and charitable; it is founded upon the immovable rock of eternal truth. Sure of the assistance of Christ for ever, sure of being directed by the spirit of truth into the one truth for ever, the holy Catholic Church has at all times condemned as heresy, any doctrine contradicting her doctrine.

As a tender mother and faithful spouse of Jesus Christ, she has always, in the spirit of charity, endeavoured to preserve her children from the delusive and flowery paths of heresy; and in the most sorrowful accents, she prays, she entreats those that have left her, to return to her pale. She perseveres in fervent prayers for the conversion of her strayed children, and would fain carry them back upon her shoulders to the only one fold of Christ. Is not this genuine charity?

Moreover, whilst the holy Catholic Church guided for ever by the Holy Ghost, fulminates her anathemas against all kinds of heresies or false doctrines, she feels nothing but charity and compassion for so many individuals born in heterodox societies. She charitably supposes several of them honest in their errors, invincibly ignorant of the true church, and consequently excusable in the sight of God. But still she deplores their misfortune of being deprived of so many means of salvation, not to be found out of her pale.

Catholic intolerance then, exhibits stronger features of genuine and practical charity, than Protestant toleration and liberality. Yet I must confess its sound is harsher, and by no means so melodious as the syren song of deception and flattery, which calls every system, *the true church of Christ,* provided it protests against the Catholic Church.

The observation made by Tertullian in his time, was, that 'the sole principle of unity amongst heretics, is the hatred of Catholicity.' The same may be truly applied to the numerous sects of the present day, which seem to have no other link of unity than their hostility to the parent church. which they have all abandoned. This seems their only rallying point, for whether we look to the Old World or the New, we will see the singular spectacle of men differing from one another in faith, as widely as earth from heaven, yet uniting in opposing that of Catholics. Nay, this animosity has long since been judged the criterion, not only of Protestant orthodoxy, but of Protestant loyalty, since the British legislature required of the members of both houses of parliament, as a necessary condition before taking their seats, to swear that they believed the Catholic worship to be superstitious, idolatrous and damnable! Provided they held this fundamental point, they were at perfect liberty to hold any other religious opinion, or none if they pleased.

CONCLUSION.

I HAVE endeavoured to explain the most essential articles of Catholic faith, in order to prove that we are not guilty of superstition, and I hope that with the candid, I have succeeded. Those who are not sincere, who with seeing eyes will not see, I cannot expect to convince. Many points of minor importance I have omitted, not wishing to swell my defence into a large volume

Thus, I have said nothing about the sign of the cross, about holy water, blessed salt, blessed candles, and many more things made use of by Catholics. It is surprising indeed, that people who call themselves christians, should be scandalized at the sign of their redemption. Freemasons have their signs, and many other societies have their signs; soldiers have their signs and countersigns; pray, why should the soldier of Jesus Christ not be permitted to arm himself with the sign of the standard of christianity, under which our chief conquered the powers of hell, and under which alone the christian soldier is to conquer? Tertullian testifies (in his book de Corona Militis) that the practice of making the sign of the cross is most ancient and most common in the church of Christ.

Pray, how will those feel, who despise and ridicule that practice, when they shall SEE THE SIGN OF THE SON OF MAN appear in heaven? Matt. xxiv. 30.

As for holy water, blessed salt, and many other things blessed by the prayers of the church, I do not understand how they can become any subject of scandal to any one believing in the power of Christ.

If inanimate things have been cursed by God's infinite justice in punishment of the sin of our first parents. (Gen. iii. 17,) that curse cannot be removed and changed into a blessing, but by the power and the merits of Jesus Christ. This supreme power, confided by Christ to his ministers, Matt. xxviii. 18, is exercised by them in blessing water, salt, and many other things, for the use of man.

Where is the superstition in believing that those elements, created for the use of man, but cursed by a justly irritated God, may be blessed again and sanctified by the prayers of the church, through the merits of Jesus Christ.

Instances are so very common of the good effects produced by the use of holy water, blessed salt, and many other blessed things, that it would take volumes to publish them all. I have been frequently applied to by parents, whose children were afflicted with the most strange and unaccountable symptoms, and have found that, after all the powers of medicine had been tried in vain, a little blessed salt, or some other things, blessed by the prayers of the church, through the merits of Jesus Christ, very often performed a complete cure.

If you were to read the memoirs of those missionaries, who, with unabated zeal, and often at the expense of their blood, converted millions of idolaters in Canada, South America, the East Indies, China, Cochin China, Siam, Persia, &c. you would find instances by hundreds, of the efficacy of the sign of the cross, holy water, &c. in banishing evil spirits, and destroying that power, which those infernal spirits frequently exercise over the souls, bodies and property of those who are guilty of idolatry, of which we find so many instances in the New Testament.

God has chosen the weak things of this world, that he might confound the strong, 1 Cor. i. 27. The efficacy of blessed things is so well known to many Protestants, that it is not very uncommon to see Protestants apply to Catholic priests for holy water, blessed salt, blessed candles, &c. To believe that any miraculous power or virtue naturally resides in that water, salt, or any other of God's inanimate creatures, would be superstition indeed, but to believe that the infinite power and goodness of Jesus Christ, exercised by the church, may apply a certain blessing to those inanimate creatures, so as to render them productive of certain happy effects, when applied to man, is no more superstition, than to believe that the waters of the Jordan, through the power of God, became instrumental in curing the leprosy of Naaman, 4 Kings v. 14.

Our age, dear sir, is the age of incredulity, commonly called the age of philosophy. It is almost fashionable to disbelieve, to reject with disdain and contempt, every thing which we cannot perceive with our carnal senses, or compass with our limited and much corrupted understanding. At the hour of death, at the entrance of eternity, when the senses shall have lost their baneful influence, and corrupted reason shall have been almost extinguished, we shall remember that God, who can do what he pleases, to whom the laws of nature are subject, who can and does, for his own glory and the salvation of man, subvert those very laws, as he did through the ministry of Moses, when he opened the Red Sea, as he did again through the ministry of Joshua, when he stopped the sun in its course. We shall then remember that there is a God of truth, who ought to be believed, who must be believed, and as much so, when what he reveals is incomprehensible, as when it is ever so plain; as much so, when what he reveals appears contrary to the laws of nature, as when his revelations are in unison with those laws.

Permit me, sir, to close my subject by contracting into as narrow a compass as possible, and exhibiting before your eyes, under one point of view, all the sublime mysteries of our creed, which have been explained to you one by one.

'I believe in God the *Father Almighty*, creator of heaven and earth.' As Father, he loves us, as God, his love to us is infinite, and as Almighty, he can do whatever he pleases, to shew his love in practice.

'And in Jesus Christ, his only Son, our Lord,'

both God and man, our only Redeemer, only as man subject to sufferings, and only as God able to satisfy God.

'Who was conceived by the Holy Ghost, born of the Virgin Mary.' Jesus Christ then was both God and man, whilst enclosed in the womb of the Virgin Mary. The Virgin Mary, is of course, the mother of Jesus Christ, both God and man, and consequently she is entitled to the highest honour which it is possible for man to exhibit to the most honourable and the most perfect of God's creatures.

'Suffered under Pontius Pilate, was crucified, dead and buried.' Suffered out of infinite love to man, the most cruel torments that the malice of hell and earth could inflict on him; suffered unto death, that we may live.

'He descended into hell; the third day he arose again from the dead.' He descended not into the hell of the damned, but as St. Peter explains it, (1 Peter, iii. 18, 19, 20,) into that prison, or place of temporal punishment, in which were detained many souls, that had departed before the coming of Christ.

'He ascended into heaven; sits at the right hand of God the Father Almighty.' There his merits are continually pleading in our behalf, there he is our high priest for ever, according to the order of Melchisedech, there he continually guides and protects his church, being with his ministers to the end of time, protecting them against the spirit of error and darkness, according to his repeated promises, Matt. xxviii. 20, John xvi. 13, &c.

'From thence he shall come to judge the living and the dead;' to give everlasting life to those who had the true faith, being members of the only true Catholic Church, and who led a holy life; and to punish with everlasting torments those who did not believe, Mark xvi. 16; those who, through their own fault, were not members of his only true Catholic Church, and those who led an ungodly life, Matt. xvi. 27.

'I believe in the Holy Ghost;' who proceeds from the Father and the Son, and is equal to them; who was promised by Jesus Christ to his church, John xiv. 26, and xvi. 13; who actually came upon the Apostles on Whitsunday, Acts ii. 1—4; who has enabled them and their successors to this day, and will enable them to the end of time, to persevere in the true and genuine doctrine of Jesus Christ, without deviating from it in one single point, John xiv. 16, 17, 18.

'The holy Catholic Church;' that church of which Jesus Christ is the architect, built upon a rock, to stand for ever, in spite of all the efforts of hell, Matt. xvi. 18, xxviii. 20; that church is *the house of the living God,* 1 Tim. iii. 15; *the kingdom of Christ,* Luke i. 33, Dan. ii. 44; *the sheep-fold of Christ,* John x. 16; *the body of which Christ is the head,* Colos. i. 18, Ephes. v. 23; *the spouse of Christ,* Ephes. v. 24—31; that church is *always subject and faithful to Christ,* Eph. v. 24; *always without spot, wrinkle or blemish, always holy,* Eph. v. 27; *always loved and cherished by him,* Ephes. v. 25, 29, Ephes. v. 31, 33; that church is *the pillar and ground of the truth,* 1 Tim. iii. 15; *always one,* Cantic. vi. 8, 9, Joan. x. 16, Ephes. iv. 4, 5; *always visible,* Isa. ii. 2, 3, Mich. iv. 1, 2, Matt. v. 14; *always and infallibly teaching the truth, the whole truth, and nothing but the truth,* Matt. xvi. 18, xxviii. 19, 20, Joan. xiv. 16, 17, 26, xvi. 13, 1 Tim. iii. 14, 15, &c. &c.

That church of course can never stand in need of reformation. The very attempt of man to reform this, the most perfect, the most noble of all the works of God, is a most daring, a most sacrilegious, most blasphemous act of impiety, of which no precedent can be found, except in the attempt made by Satan to equal himself to the Most High, for which he was precipitated into the eternal abyss. This holy Catholic Church is spread over the universe, which makes it *Catholic,* teaching every where the same doctrine, because she is wholly inspired and directed by the holy spirit of truth, John xiv. 16, 17, 26, and always guided by Christ, Matt xxviii. 20. The ministers of that church form but one body, of which St. Peter and his successors were by divine authority constituted heads, Matt. xvi. 18, 19, Luke xxii. 32, Joan: xxi. 15, 16, 17.

'The communion of saints.' In the church of God, there is a communion of its members in holy things, being partakers of the same spiritual blessings, sacraments, &c. which Christ empowered his church to administer. We likewise communicate with the blessed saints in heaven. They are already landed on the shores of eternal peace. We are yet tossed by the raging billows of a tempestuous sea. We stretch out our hands to them for help; we beg their intercession to obtain a safe landing. We meditate on their virtues; we are encouraged by their examples; we confide much in their charitable intercession, Revel. v. 8, Zach. i. 12. 2, Macchab. xv. 12—14, Tob. xii. 12, Heb. i. 14, Rev. ii. 26, 27, Luc. xv. 10, Mat. xviii. 10, &c. Whilst we look up to the saints in heaven for their help and assistance, we offer up our prayers and intercession for those of our fellow-members, who having died before they had fully satisfied the justice of God, have yet to suffer for a time, before they can be admitted into that sanctuary where nothing defiled can enter, 1 Cor. iii. 15, 1 Pet. iii. 18—20.

'The forgiveness of sins.' This forgiveness of sins, originating in the infinite power and mercy of God alone, and granted solely in consideration of the merits of Christ, is administered to us by the ministers of Christ in the holy Catholic Church, first in the sacrament of baptism; and then again in the sacrament of penance, upon our sincere repentance and conversion, and upon sincere confession, Matt. xviii. 18, John xx. 22. 23. Acts xix. 18, James v. 16, &c.

'The resurrection of the body, and life everlasting, Amen.' A glorious resurrection of soul and body, by which we are to become members of the church triumphant of Jesus Christ, will be granted to those only, who have been true members of the only one and true church militant of Christ on earth. And those who had not the holy Catholic Church, the spouse of Christ, for their mother, will find to their everlasting sorrow, that they have not Jesus Christ for their Father and Saviour.

Permit me now, dear sir, to address you in the spirit of charity, and to entreat you to meditate seriously on the following solemn truths:—

The day is fast approaching, when you and I will be summoned before the dreaded tribunal of Jesus Christ; I, in the capacity of a Roman Catholic priest; you, in the capacity of a Protestant minister; both claiming the title of minister of Christ. What will become of that one, who shall not be able then to substantiate his claim, and to establish his title. We may be suffered by a God of infinite mercy and patience, to establish the most unfounded, the most extravagant titles before men; but will the illusion be suffered to continue before the tribunal of eternal justice? And will not the bright rays of pure and undefiled truth forever dissipate those foul and thick mists of corruption, which in this world enabled us to dupe ourselves and others? Will not the two-edged sword of truth cut off all those difficulties, which our own corruption had raised as a bulwark against the authenticated revelations of Jesus Christ? Will not the bright and dazzling rays of glory, that shall emanate from the throne of the Omnipotent Judge, be the most incontestable proof of the divinity of his revelation, and of the truth of those mysteries, against which proud and corrupted reason suggested so many difficulties?

When the sacred code shall be opened, by which all christians are to be tried, will it be permitted there, think you, to allege the foolish dictates of human philosophy, in opposition to the plain revelations of that sacred code? Will it be permitted there, to talk about reforming the most noble work of the great God? Will it be permitted there, (by way of apology,) to tell Jesus Christ, that he broke his repeated promises? That he had promised to be with his church to the end of time, and yet that he had forsaken that church and permitted it to go astray? That he had promised the spirit of truth to it to guide it into all the truth for ever, yet he had withdrawn that spirit of truth, and permitted the church to become a sink of errors and idolatry? Will it be permitted there, to call the plain ordinances of Jesus Christ, Papist superstitions? Will it be permitted there, (by way of apology for not complying with his ordinances,) to tell Jesus Christ that such and such things were impossible? That no man could forgive sin, not even those, who most plainly and distinctly had received that power from him? Will you be permitted there, think you, to tell Jesus Christ to his face, that it was impossible for him to give his flesh and blood under the appearance of bread and wine? Will you there be permitted to allege the testimony of your corrupted senses and limited reason, in opposition to the plain and repeated assertions of Infinite Wisdom? Will it be permitted there, think you, in the face of the cross, that sign of the Son of Man, to ridicule those, who signed themselves with that holy sign? In short, sir, will it be permitted there, to deceive yourself and others any longer? Corrupted reason sat upon the tribunal in this world, and with more than Satanic presumption, summoned before it the tremendous mysteries clearly and distinctly revealed by an Omnipotent God, to be judged, to be approved or condemned, according to its own whimsical notions, and more so according to its corrupt inclinations. The case will be then reversed, infinite power and wisdom will occupy the judgment seat; proud reason, with all its boast of philosophy, will stand confused, appalled, convicted, and be forever silenced. Will it be permitted to say, by way of apology, I rejected such and such mysteries, because I could not understand them, or because they appeared to me impossible? But, you were not required to understand them, you were only commanded to listen and adore; and this you could have done as easily, as so many millions of persons, as wise as yourself. Ah! sir, believe me, believe a person, who is sincerely concerned for the salvation of your soul; the very garb which at present is considered by you as a mark of distinction and honour, will, before the dreadful tribunal, on the day of God's eternal vengeance, be the terror and despair of your soul, and its everlasting condemnation; I mean the garb of Protestantism. You protested! Against what? Against the church of Christ! Against divine ordinances! Against divine and tremendous mysteries. Against all that is sacred! This was not enough. Under the title of minister of Christ, you taught thousands to do the same, to ridicule and blaspheme what they did not understand, and by misrepresenting the holy mysteries of the Catholic Church, you prevented their return to that only sheep-fold of Christ, from which the pride and corruption of some arch-heretics of former times caused their ancestors to depart. Thousands and thousands of these unfortunate lay-people will have a lawful excuse to allege before the tribunal of impartial justice, namely, the misrepresentation of their teachers. Many of them will find their acquittal in the plea of invincible ignorance. Will this plea be of any avail to those who with seeing eyes would not see? To those, who, without mission from above, without deputation from the Catholic Church of Christ, presumed to step into the sanctuary, and to arrogate to themselves that sacred title, which the Catholic Church alone can give, she being exclusively the depository of the power of Jesus Christ on earth?

For God's sake, dear sir, if you value the glory of God, and the salvation of your soul, give up protesting against the Catholic Church; in it alone you will find salvation. As sure as God lives, it is the true church of Christ. May the day of judgment be for me the day of God's eternal vengeance, if the Roman Catholic Church is not the only one true and immaculate spouse of Christ. May my soul be doomed to suffer for you to all eternity, all those torments, which you would deserve by following all the pretended superstitions of the church of Rome.

Hush into silence your prejudices; listen and adore; humble yourself with St. Paul to the very dust; pray for light, and you shall see it brighter than the dazzling rays of the mid-day's sun. Ask for grace to overcome human respect and all carnal considerations, those obstacles which Satan raises to prevent the conversion of millions; that grace will be imparted to you. Seek the kingdom of heaven, by which in Scripture language, is often meant the church of Christ, the Catholic Church, as yet in a state of suffering, persecuted, ridiculed, tried like gold in the furnace, as yet wandering through the dreary and frightful desert, but on its way to the land of promise; you will find it, and with it you will enter the mansions of eternal peace. That you and all your hearers may obtain that blessing of blessings, is the sincere desire, and shall be the constant prayer of

  Your humble and obedient servant,
    DEMETRIUS A. GALLITZIN

AN APPEAL
TO THE PROTESTANT PUBLIC

Religious controversies, when carried on in the spirit of charity, and with candour, are certainly of great utility; as they tend to dispel the clouds of error which obscure or deform the truth, and to unite those whom a diversity of opinion keeps at variance. Unfortunately, however, for the cause of religion, religious controversies do not often proceed from a spirit of charity, and are but seldom expressed in the sweet accents of harmonious suavity, in consequence of which, the breach is made wider.

When I published my 'Defence of Catholic Principles,' I was actuated by charity and zeal for the salvation of my brethren in Christ, and I did not intentionally make use of any expression calculated to hurt the feelings of any. I was not the aggressor, but compelled by duty to repel the rude and unprovoked attacks of an enemy of our holy religion. I find by his late publication that he is one of those

>'Who prove their doctrine orthodox,
>By apostolic blows and knocks.'

For this reason, and for some others which I am

now going to state, I shall not address any more letters to the 'Protestant Minister,' but direct my future publications on religious subjects, 'to a Protestant friend.'

The Protestant Minister, has spent nearly two years in gathering and publishing his 'Vindication,' in which he endeavours to exhibit Roman Catholics to the eyes of the public as a superstitious and idolatrous people; and I must own, that in the execution of his design, he has acquired a claim on the gratitude of the whole body of Catholics, and especially of the Catholic clergy—having furnished us with new proofs of the weakness of his cause, and of the impossibility of overthrowing, by fair argument, the principles of Catholics.

The most solid arguments by which I have established our principles, he has not ventured to attack, but passed them unnoticed—knowing them to be unanswerable.

He has generally attached himself to some of the weakest proofs only, which I had adduced in favour of our principles; but which alone, would not be sufficient to establish them.

In my defence of 'Catholic Principles,' have attached myself to the most essential points of religion only; those on which depends your salvation. And the proofs on which I have established these fundamental points, are principally taken from Scripture. Many of you, my Protestant brethren, have been candid enough to acknowledge that these proofs are unanswerable, and leave no chance for a reply. Convinced by these arguments, and giving way to the grace of God, some few among you have applied to me, and testified an eager desire to renounce their errors, and become members of the Catholic Church. What does the Protestant Minister do? In order to draw your attention from the main subject, he introduces numbers of subjects of minor importance, which he exhibits in the most odious colours, and in all the ludicrous shapes of low ribaldry.

Although he denies the existence of infallibility, in the whole body of Catholic prelates, yet he seems to claim that infallibility for himself: for how can he otherwise expect that the least respect or attention can be due to his interpretations of Scripture, especially when he takes the liberty to take hold of the sacred text, as he would a nose of wax, and squeeze it into whatever shape he pleases, to make it answer his purpose. In reading his 'Vindication,' you must have admired his ingenuity, as an interpreter of Scripture.

'The gates of hell shall not prevail against the church,' Matt. xvi. 'That means,' says he, page 14, 'that death shall not prevail against the genuine members of the church.'

'Unless you eat the flesh of the Son of man, and drink his blood, you shall not have life in you.' John vi. 'This means,' says he, page 24, 'that we must believe in Christ.'

'This is my body,' &c. 'This is my blood,' &c. 'That means,' says the Protestant Minister, 'This is *not* my body, this is *not* my blood—for it is nothing but bread and wine,' page 27, 28.

'Receive ye the Holy Ghost; whose sins you shall forgive, they are forgiven,' &c. John xx. 22, 23. That means nothing at all, 'for,' says the Protestant Minister, page 19, 'where is that power (of forgiving sins) given to a sinful creature, and one who has to answer for his own sins?'

Jesus said, 'Son be of good cheer, thy sins are forgiven thee,' Matt. ix. 'That means only,' says the same minister, page 20, 'that the temporal punishment of sin was released.'

'The church of the living God,' says St. Paul, 1 Tim. iii. 15, 'is the pillar and ground of truth.' 'That means,' says the Protestant Minister, pages 15, 16, 'only the church of Ephesus.'

Christ says, 'Blessed are they that have not seen and have believed,' John xx. 29. That means nothing; for the minister tells you, page 29, 'that the foundation of our faith must rely on the truth of our senses.'

The Apostle St. Paul, says, 'if any man's work burn, he shall suffer loss, but he himself shall be saved, yet so as by fire,' 1 Cor. iii. 15. 'That means,' says the Protestant Minister, 'yet so as out of the fire,' page 47.

I freely confess, my dear brethren, that I am no match for the Protestant Minister; for he hath the Holy Scripture at his command, can squeeze it into any shape, or make it say what he pleases; he therefore, can never be at a loss. I, on the contrary, am so convinced of my ignorance, of my inability to interpret Scripture, that I in all cases, confine myself to that interpretation which the Holy Catholic Church gives me: because my Saviour Christ has promised, that the Spirit of Truth shall remain with his Apostles *forever*, John xiv. 16, 17. And because Christ, when he sent his Apostles, to begin the work of the ministry, preaching, baptizing, &c. &c. promised to be and remain with them until the consummation of the world, Matt. xxviii. 20. And finally, because the same Christ, the Divine Architect, who built the church, built it upon a rock, and promised that the gates of hell should not prevail against it. Matt. xvi. 18. The sense of which declaration is explained by Christ himself, Matt. vii. 25, where speaking of a house raised by a wise man, he says, 'it fell not, for it was founded upon a rock.' Now I am so confident that Christ has kept all these promises, that I feel perfectly happy and safe in taking the Catholic Church as my only guide in the interpretation of the Holy Scripture and in all matters of salvation. Thus I am confined within certain narrow limits beyond which I cannot step, and therefore am no match for the Protestant Minister, who is not constrained by any limits whatever; for he tells us plainly, and repeatedly, that *the Scriptures alone*, no matter how interpreted, for every one is to interpret for himself, as well as he can, are our only rule of faith.

This is not all. I do not wish to give the gentleman any offence, or to hurt his feelings, knowing that charity is the principal virtue of a christian, nay, the very soul of religion. However, truth being the sole object of a writer, who undertakes to defend the true religion, he is of course obliged to point out the many misrepresentations by which it is deformed, and the falsehoods by which it is rendered hateful or ridiculous. To perform this task is highly unpleasant; as zeal for the cause of truth, which animates the writer, may easily be mistaken for malice or ill-will. God knows I feel nothing but charity for the Protestant Minister. His endeavours in misrepresenting the Catholic doctrine, the odium and ridicule he throws on the Catholic clergy, by representing them as impostors, sorcerers, slight of hand men, cruel executioners, blood-suckers, roasting the bodies of men, &c. &c. excites in me nothing but compassion, and a fervent desire that God may open his eyes before it is too late.

I would fain wish to persuade myself that he errs through ignorance, in which case I certainly should address a second letter to him, in order to undeceive him; but no, I am compelled to believe, that he wilfully and knowingly advances falsehoods in order to render the Catholic religion hateful and ridiculous, and establish his own system. You, my dear brethren, will be able to judge whether I be right or wrong. I shall at present only mention a few of the most palpable falsehoods advanced by the Protestant Minister, intending to be more particular in my future publications.

Page 20. He tells you that 'the Pope and his priests think it no blasphemy * * * * * * * * * * * to thrust the souls of men into purgatory, and either to roast them there for hundreds of years, or, if their friends are rich enough, to bring them out in a shorter time.'

As the Protestant Minister has read the Catholic doctrine of purgatory, he, of course, knows the lines quoted above to be false.

Page 75. He tells you that our holy water 'is composed of water, salt, a live coal put into it, and the priest's spittle.'

As the minister tells us, page 140, he is acquainted with the missal or mass-book, which contains the blessing of the water, he therefore is guilty of a wilful falsehood in the above assertion. He is guilty of telling no less a falsehood, when he tells you, page 140, 'that the Catholic priests have with all their might endeavoured to suppress all attempts of translating the Roman mass-book, breviary,' &c. &c.

Thousands of English prayer-books, used by the Catholics of America, and hundreds of thousands by the Catholics of England, Ireland and Scotland, contain the whole mass, word by word, in the English language; and there are besides other books printed for lay people, which contain in the English language, all the different masses and offices for the most solemn days and times of the year, such as Advent, Lent, Holy Week, Easter Week, Pentecost, &c. translated from the Roman mass-book and breviary. Many more such translations are to be found in the hands of Catholics living in Catholic countries, such as France, Spain, Portugal, Italy, the greater part of Germany, &c. &c.

I have translations of the kind in both English and French, and I do most solemnly call upon you, my dear brethren, to produce any one person among yourselves, who understands French and Latin, and I shall in order to satisfy you, give him a chance to compare said translations with the original Latin mass-book. This will also give you an opportunity of finding out how horribly the Protestant Minister imposes on you, and with how little conscience he calumniates the Catholic Church, when he speaks, page 140, of *'the filth and abominable corruption'* contained in our massbooks,' &c. and 'hid under the cover of an unknown tongue.'

How much will you be surprised when you shall find that nearly nine-tenths of the contents of the mass-book and breviary are taken from the Holy Scriptures, and that the remainder is a short account of the holy lives of some of the principal saints, proposed for imitation, together with some prayers to obtain their intercession with Almighty God, that we may be enabled to follow their steps, and thus to be admitted to enjoy, in partnership with them, the blessings of eternal life.

Page 104. The minister in laying before you the Catholic creed, as published by Pope Pius IV. has the following words:

'I do believe that the saints reigning together with Christ are to be *worshipped* and prayed unto.' And again, pretending to quote the Council of Trent; 'the sacred bodies of martyrs, &c. are to be *worshipped*.'

Here again is a wilful corruption. The Roman ritual which contains the said creed or profession of faith for receiving converts into the church, does not say *worshipped* but *honoured*. 'That the saints reigning together with Christ, are to be *honoured*,' &c. I pledge my word to you, dear brethren, to shew you these words in the Roman ritual any time you apply to me. The Council of Trent does not say that the sacred bodies of martyrs, &c. are to be *worshipped* but *venerated*, as having been in this life, according to St. Paul, 1 Cor. iii. 16, 17, 'temples of the Holy Ghost,' and according to the same, 1 Cor. vi. 15, 'members of Christ.' What shall I say of the minister's assertion, page 100, that 'the church allows not only the deposing but also the killing of crowned heads.' I hope you will forgive me, my dear brethren, if I denominate this a most wicked malicious lie, invented by Satan, the father of lies, and his ministers, to lead you astray from the Holy Catholic Church.

I shall not at present pollute my pages with any more of the Protestant Minister's misrepresentations and falsehoods; they shall all be noticed in due time. Let me here only remark, that as those falsehoods are generally advanced without any proof, they of course ought to bear no weight. It is a general principle of law and justice, that every person is to be considered innocent until proved guilty. And the more heinous the crime is, with which a person is charged, the stronger the proofs ought to be before he can be considered guilty. This principle is not admitted by the Pro-

'testant Minister; his most fixed determination is to raise the utmost hatred against the Catholic Church, and to render it ridiculous and contemptible. And in order to accomplish his design, he charges the church with all the crimes committed by some of its members.

So, because Clement and Ravaillac, two monsters in human flesh, were guilty of murdering two French kings, he tells you it is the principle of the Catholic Church to murder kings.

So, likewise, page 63, because certain ignorant friars wrote that 'even God himself is subject to the Virgin Mary, and such like blasphemies,' therefore he tells you that the Catholic Church approves and teaches those blasphemies.

What would you think of me, my friends, if I should assert that the Protestant religion approves of murder; for a certain Protestant minister murdered one of his elders some years ago in Bedford. Or, if I should assert that the said religion approves of drunkenness, for some of its members, and even some of its ministers, are in the habit of getting drunk.

Unfortunately, there are too many members of the Catholic Church, whose conduct widely differs from their speculative principles; who have nothing of Christians but the name; and who are capable of committing the most atrocious crimes. The church condemns their conduct, admonishes them to repent, denounces to them the judgments of God, if they do not repent, but she is not invested with the power to compel their amendment.

The Protestant Minister shews a particular want of generosity in his lengthy account of the wickedness and extravagant claims of some of the Popes. After the acknowledgment and concession I have made on that subject, pages 147—157 of my 'Defence,' he ought to have been ashamed to say even one word on the subject. The prevarications of Popes can no more be charged to the church, than the treason of Judas or the fall of St. Peter; and therefore if all his assertions against our Popes were true, this would be no argument against the Catholic Church. Throughout the whole of the minister's 'Vindication,' I find a total want of sincerity and candour, a perversion and misrepresentation of my arguments, and the most sedulous and persevering endeavours to bury the fundamental and essential tenets of Catholic faith under a load of irrelevant matter.

As an instance of his want of sincerity, and I must add, of a gross imposition on the public, I beg leave to refer you to page 9, line 29, of the 'Vindication,' where the minister tries to make you believe that I said 'Scripture should not be read,' whereas he very well knows that I only said that Holy Writ, (although certainly God's word) was not intended to be our supreme judge in matters of faith &c. &c.

Where he could not by any solid arguments overthrow the Catholic doctrine itself, he has only attacked its abuses, for which the church cannot be made answerable; for the most holy things have been, and will be abused. He has made use of vile and scurrilous language, unworthy a christian and a gentleman, of which I need not give here any particular instance.

He has wilfully perverted the words of our general councils and the sense of our doctrine, in order to make it ridiculous and contemptible.

He has even perverted the meaning of plain English words, to answer the same purpose, trying to make you believe that to *venerate* signifies *worship*, &c.

He has been guilty of advancing most palpable falsehoods, as in the case of the holy water, &c.

He has carefully, and in very many instances, concealed from your view most essential parts of the truth.

Finally, such are his anger and ill-will against Catholics, that he cannot bring himself to call them by their proper name. Nothing will do for him but Papists, Romanists, Romish, in the true style of British statutes.

These are a few of my reasons for not addressing any more of my letters to the Protestant minister.

Should he ever be willing hereafter to recall the many falsehoods he has advanced; to confute by solid arguments the Catholic principles; to do it in a decorous manner, in a manner becoming a christian and a gentleman, without comparing the Pope to an old cow, without calling the priests impostors, sorcerers, conjurors, &c. without introducing irrelevant matters, such as the scandalous conduct of some Popes, &c. I shall then consider it my duty to resume the correspondence with the Protestant Minister. And I believe that a controversy carried on in a mild dispassionate way, proceeding on both sides from a spirit of charity, attacking only principles, not men, would go a great way towards dispelling the clouds of error that have too long obscured the truth, would silence the spirit of bigotry and malevolence, and would re-unite in the bonds of charity those whom the infernal spirit of religious discord, often mistaken for religious zeal, has too long kept at variance.

My brethren, we are all the children of God. We are all brothers and sisters in Jesus Christ. Let us for ever banish hatred and malice from our hearts, and be guided only by the Spirit of Truth and Charity which Jesus Christ sent to his Apostles and disciples, which formed them into *one* church, and which Christ promised should remain with them until the consummation of the world.

www.ingramcontent.com/pod-product-compliance
Lightning Source LLC
Chambersburg PA
CBHW032226230426
43666CB00033B/1602